More Muck And Less Money

Further Humorous Tales from a Cumbrian Farm

Joyce Wilson

Best Wishes?

Joyce Wilson

SEATALLAN

Published by Seatallan Press
6 Downfield Lane, Bigrigg, Egremont,
Cumbria CA22 2UY

First published 1995

Typeset in 10^1/$_2$/12pt Meridien by
Deltatype Ltd, Ellesmere Port, Cheshire
Printed and bound in Great Britain by
Athenæum Press Ltd, Gateshead, Tyne & Wear

British Library Cataloguing in Publication Data
A catalogue record for this book is available
from the British Library

ISBN 0-9528919-9-9
(previously published by Ellenbank Press, Park Hill South,
Camp Road, Maryport Cumbria CA15 6JN under
ISBN 1-873551-07-X)

CONTENTS

To my husband, Joe

1

DELIVERING WOOL

'Are you still milking that bloody cow, Bill?'

'She's not used to being wakened as early as this, Dad. She's bad enough when she's ready to get up. Just look! Her tail's swinging about like a racing pendulum clock.'

'It's you who should be racing a bit more. I told Seth Foster you'd be in his yard by six o'clock, ready to load up his fleeces . . . A bloody nuisance, the whole thing . . . I don't know why folk read the *Whitehaven News* so closely anyway. Most of them have never been to Ravenglass.'

'What on earth are you talking about, Dad? What has reading the paper got to do with delivering a few fleeces of wool to Ravenglass Station?'

'Because there was an advert offering a better price for wool in Bradford, and this quick-thinking firm worded it all so well that most of the neighbours around here think it's a good idea.'

'I notice you loaded *our* few bags last night!'

'Well, I have my doubts about the whole thing. But, as I'd offered our horse and cart to take the load to Ravenglass Station, I reckoned I might as well give it a try.'

'Why did you volunteer to collect the wool if you weren't interested?'

'I felt sorry for old Seth. He has no help on that little farm – no son or daughter, and only one old horse that would never make such a journey and he was so keen to try something a bit new . . . So I said it would be no trouble for you to collect the wool. A young chap like you will enjoy a journey like that. It's educational for you to see a bit more of the country . . . When I was your age I had to walk on my own two feet if I wanted to see anything, not ride comfortably behind a good horse . . . You don't know you're born!'

'I notice that there are another three farms to call at and collect wool, all inconveniently placed down lonnings, well off the beaten track. Besides, there's a dance in Bootle tonight, and Len's giving me a lift in his car, so I don't want to be late home.

'All the way to Bootle, and you're complaining about a few miles to Ravenglass with a lively horse! A lot of them second-hand cars break down . . . At least Captain won't come to a dead stop. I can't understand folk going to see a concert in such an out of the way spot. There must be a woman in the picture somewhere. No doubt she'll be impressed when a chap turns up in a fancy motor car.'

'There's no woman involved, Dad. Len plays the trumpet in the band, so I said I'd go with to keep him company. He's not sure of the road.'

'And when were you ever in Bootle?'

'Never, but two of us can find the way better than one.'

Jackson got up from his milking and nodded his head reflectively.

'Yes, Seth is a good example of the wrong person reading the *Whitehaven News*.'

He made his way to the byre door still muttering to himself, as Bill walked towards a quiet little black Aberdeen Angus cow that was easy to milk, amazed that his father had overlooked this pleasant little animal.

'Come on Nell, move over before he comes back.' Nell hadn't long to go before she calved again, so her yield was decreasing rapidly each day. Not much milk here, thought Bill, hoping his father would return and choose one of the more difficult cows to milk before he'd finished Nell.

Opposite he could see Mollie's eyes fixed on him. He had heard the jealous rattle of her chain as he'd settled to milk the little black cow. Even the dozing Maud had raised a weary eyelid as he had passed by her stall. Getting up at half-past five on a dark cold autumn morning was bad

enough without having to face these two temperamental beasts. Saved! He heard the byre door open, then close, making the paraffin lamp sway drunkenly from its nail.

Bill eyed his father from the comfortable vantage point of Nell's flank.

Good! He was approaching the neurotic Maud. Bill's day was made – of all his father's herd, Maud was the only one he truly hated. Small teats and cloven hooves always at the ready!

Jackson casually threw a scoop of cowcake into Maud's trough before settling down to milk her.

Bill fumed silently. Why didn't Maud play any of her pranks when Jackson milked her? There's no justice, he thought to himself.

'The cause of all the trouble with Seth Foster,' continued the old farmer, as though his train of thought hadn't been interrupted, 'as I said, is the *Whitehaven News*.'

'You can't blame the paper for the adverts that are printed in it,' Bill pointed out. 'Everybody has a choice. It's up to them to ignore what they read.'

'You young folk know nowt these days,' retorted Jackson, giving the restless Maud a sharp shove. 'And you can stop your dancing about, Milady. I don't have time this morning for any of your carry on,' he snapped in Maud's direction.

Instant stillness and attention was the result – much to Bill's disappointment.

Jackson continued. 'You youngsters don't realise that there was a time when ordinary folk weren't taught how to read, and so they were satisfied with the local market. Nowadays they can find nothing better to do than sit by the fire with a copy of the *Whitehaven News* or the *Farmers' Weekly*, looking for something new to spend their money on.'

'Seth Foster has plenty of common sense – he's always struck me as a clever chap.'

'That's what I mean, he's too well-educated. Chaps like him always listened to the teacher at school, so they think everything they see in print is the gospel truth. No, no, he would have been a more thinking chap if he'd spent a few sunny afternoons on the beach looking for crabs or laying set-lines, learning how to feed himself, instead of always reading somebody else's second-hand ideas.'

'Good God! He's only selling a couple of fleeces. What has that got to do with playing truant at school?'

'Using your own intelligence, that's what I'm talking about. I read that advert myself – it sounded as though there was a fortune waiting just round the corner for us Cumbrian farmers if we'd only go to the trouble of sending our wool to Bradford. Isn't that in Yorkshire?'

'Yes, it is.'

'Isn't that where them Swaledales come from?'

'I suppose it is.'

'Well, if they haven't enough wool of their own then there must be something funny about it all.'

'Didn't it say in the advert that they require more wool, owing to an increased demand for cloth?'

'Well, we'll see about that . . . Are you going to milk yon newly calved cow over there? Or are you content to watch the milk trickling from her tits all over the byre floor? Anybody with any sense would have milked her first. It's a right do when a father has to tell his son every little detail. I've even noticed a couple of cats at the top of the byre waiting their chance. They'll be under the cow's belly licking up the milk before you get there. At least *they* can't bear to see good milk running to waste.'

Bill made his way to the roan cow his father had indicated, wishing he dared answer him back now and again. But that wouldn't be any use anyway, as his father always had an answer ready. Perhaps when he'd lived a bit longer he would be able to think of something to take the ground from under the old man's feet. He sat down and began to milk the distended udder. This cow gave so much milk he would be last in for breakfast and he could already hear his father complaining that he would be late setting out for Ravenglass. The only thing he was pleased about was that he was allowed to take Captain the Shire-cross horse, who would eat up the miles and get him back in good time to meet Len. It was a pity he had to go back towards Gosforth to collect Ned Rothery's wool before he turned again to pass their own gate on the way to Ravenglass. God! How heavy this bucket of milk was . . . And the cow still had another bucketful inside her. He knew he would be tired before he even set off.

* * *

As Bill drove the lively Captain out through the farm gate, his father stood ready to close it after them.

'And don't chase the guts out of that good horse. I want

9

him to work for the rest of the week, with all his feet sound. Not like he was when you went for that load of coal to Drigg last year. I had to have him reshod before he could do a decent day's work!'

Bill gritted his teeth, wishing he dared to remind his cantakerous father that he had pointed out the slack shoe for a good week before he had gone for the coal, and that he'd had to nurse the horse and load home, knowing he would be blamed. He heaved a sigh of relief as the powerful gelding pulled the light load easily on to the main road. Now he was out of sight of the old man – free as a bird – and could enjoy the day's journey.

Mrs Rothery, kind as ever, gave him a mug of tea and a slice of currant cake even though he had only just left home. 'You'll feel hungry, lad, before you get far along the road,' she said, glad to see a visitor so early in the morning.

Captain passed their own gateway very reluctantly, as Bill made his way south, his cart already a bit heavier, loaded with a few more bags of wool. Once Captain realised that his journey wasn't to be a short one, he settled his shoulders into the collar and stepped out smartly, his eyes scanning the fields alongside the main road for signs of life.

Other horses always gave a friendly whinny to passers-by, and there was always a chance that his master would stop to have a crack with other farmers, allowing Captain to steal a tasty bite of grass. He could never understand why his master always made him walk past all the fresh grass which grew along the sides of the roads, but released him in the evening into a field which all the other stock had been busy nibbling all day. If he, Peggy and Dolly were allowed to graze the roadsides he was sure they would all be able to pull these silly wheels along much quicker. Humans, he supposed, who never seemed to eat any grass anyway, couldn't be expected to understand these important matters.

He also realised that he would be treated to fewer stops

with this driver, who never paused to chat to other humans like his father did. No, today would come to a quick end if he just moved on as fast as he could, and at least this load was a pleasure to pull . . . Oh, but where was he going now? Turning down this nasty little lonning, just when he had got into his stride. Never mind, there might be a bite and a drink at the next farm, just like the last one.

'Here you are then, Bill. I'm glad you can take my load for me. You're a grand lad. Would you like to come in for a while, it's just on coffee time?'

Bill could see the day passing before his eyes. Would he ever make it back in time to go to Bootle tonight? However, he knew his father would be annoyed at his lack of friendliness if he refused the offer of a snack; having such a sociable father had certain disadvantages.

As he pulled out on to the main road an hour later, Bill glanced across the fields to his father's farmhouse, thinking how, after over an hour of travelling and loading, to say nothing of the chatting and coffee breaks, he had barely left home. Captain, of course, thought the day's work was over and gleefully tried to turn left at the end of Hall Senna lonning, only to be disillusioned for the second time that morning.

'Come on Captain, only one more stop before we reach Ravenglass. It's just a pity the old man met so many other farmers at the auction – most of them living in out of the way spots – who fancied selling their wool to some greedy chap from Bradford . . . Come to think of it, they probably met in one of the pubs in Preston Street. I reckon there's more business done in the pubs than there is in the auction itself.'

Captain tossed his head as if to say, 'He's telling me something, so I'd better give some sort of sign that I know he's still sitting up there.'

Bill was perched on the front ledge of the cart, his feet on the left-hand shaft, a thick pullover folded beneath him to make the seat more comfortable. Captain had a good crisp stride, unlike the more ladylike Peggy who had become used to Jackson's slow walking pace. She was his father's favourite and resented any attempt to speed her up. She also chose to stop at the door of every pub in the district! He was sure his father knew if another driver had tried to hurry the mare along . . . Maybe there was some sort of telepathy between them?

The sharp slap of Captain's shoes on the tarmac road seemed to count out the seconds. How many more to Ravenglass? He looked along the horse's dark back as it moved under the harness, young and strong, fast for a horse, but slow to the impatient Bill. Some young farm workers encouraged these young horses to trot, but he daren't; his father would know. No, he would have to be patient and enjoy the strange countryside.

Holmrook, with its steep descent to the river and the faithful fishermen who clustered hopefully round the edge of the bank pool, soon lay before him. He would have liked to spend more time admiring the lovely salmon lying beside one of the luckier anglers. His catch had encouraged the group to tend their rods with more enthusiasm.

Captain didn't like waiting while Bill went into the shop to buy a few sweets. Why does he have to stop where there is no grazing? thought the annoyed horse. *He* seems to be enjoying a bite of something, but he doesn't think about me. He tossed his head to let Bill know he was displeased.

'I know you don't like waiting in front of shops, Captain, but we'll soon reach the last farm on our list. Then it's straight to the station . . . Come on.'

A shake of the reins and the block cart was rattling towards the bridge.

Having collected the last two bales, the horse and cart turned left again on to the Ravenglass road.

'This is countryside I don't know at all, Captain,' Bill said in the general direction of the two dark ears which momentarily twitched, monitoring the tenor of his speech. Once he'd ascertained that Bill was only talking to himself, Captain returned his ears to the best position for listening for sounds ahead. Perhaps they'd meet another horse around the next corner?

His hooves sounded loud as they walked under the arch of trees which almost met above them. 'What a strange place!' thought Captain. The sounds of small animals and birds in the woods nearby held his attention . . . Today was turning out to be a nice change from the usual trailing up and down in one of his master's fields. Then he snorted, and the sound almost made him jump as it echoed through the tunnel of trees.

'Carleton Hall,' read Bill aloud as they passed the entrance to a large house on the left.

'And now a road junction!' he said to Captain a few steps later.

'Let's see what this sign says.' The horse had already stopped. Perhaps Bill had decided that this walk had taken them far enough from home.

'To the left Ravenglass, two miles, on the main road . . . To the right Ravenglass via Saltcoats, one mile, along a very narrow road . . . That's a funny sign. How can there be two distances to Ravenglass? The main road is obviously for cars and lorries, and this little road must be quicker and used for farm traffic.'

Captain's ears switched their frequency while he rested a hind leg on the toe of its hoof, waiting for Bill to make up his mind.

'Yes, Captain. I reckon this little road is ours. It isn't suitable for very heavy traffic, and our load doesn't come into that category . . . and I'm late enough as it is.'

Bill shook the reins briskly across the unwilling back, and the load moved forward. He felt much happier. This was the right decision and with a bit of luck he would be on his way home in no time at all.

Bill could enjoy his ride now, he gazed around from his vantage point on top of the cart – quiet road, no motor cars or lorries overtaking him. Captain was swinging along comfortably, his hoofbeats ringing out a pleasant rhythm.

'Hello! What's this?' Just a level crossing, with the keeper's house close by . . . Thankfully the gates were open, saving Bill from calling on the keeper's wife to leave her work.

Captain pulled the cart effortlessly over the double track, and they were off again. It couldn't be far now . . . he could smell the seaweed . . . and taste the salt on his lips. Surely just round the next corner. . .

Here we are, a farm on the right . . . and . . . another one in the distance.

They passed the last farm and Bill gasped in amazement as he caught sight of the estuary. He pulled the horse to a sudden stop, eager to spend a few minutes contemplating one of the most magnificent and unexpected views he had ever seen.

Swooping terns, swirling black-headed gulls, and searching oystercatchers squawked in excitement as they hunted food along the thin slow-moving river which drifted reluctantly towards its journey's end. To his right a few fishing boats waited for the incoming tide to rescue them from their perches on the shore, masts and rigging leaning wherever the receding tide had carelessly abandoned them. Looking further south, Bill recognised the distinctive outline of Black Combe, the most westerly of mountains, crouched like a guard dog waiting to vet any traveller who might choose to enter or leave this distant coastal strip of England.

What a strange place! Beautiful, shimmering in the afternoon sunlight. A corner of Cumberland bypassed by a hurrying twentieth century, thought Bill to himself as he eased the horse forward.

The road stopped at the farm, but a firm sandy track led on, skirting a high boundary wall built to keep the incoming tide at bay. The horse followed the track marked by a row of up-ended, tarred railway sleepers leading to the now visible village of Ravenglass.

Bill could see the houses lining the far side of the estuary. He spotted the railway station high up, while here on his left was a bridge where the railway line crossed the river. The arches of the bridge framed an astonishing view of the Wasdale peaks. Scafell and the Screes were clearly highlighted in the afternoon sun.

Captain's hooves clinked on the pebbly path, disturbing some sheep who were drinking fresh water from ruts formed by the wheels of countless carts. The path began to shelve very gently towards the river.

'Good God! It's a ford!' gasped Bill. 'A bloody ford!'

The horse leaned back into his harnes to slow his load down. Bill could see the tide just pushing its first tiny waves inland across the surface of the fresh water.

'Thank goodness I can still get across. I daren't think how much time I would have wasted if I'd had to go all the way back to the crossroads', he said to himself as he urged the big horse into the water.

An encouraging slap across his hindquarters and Captain settled his neck into the collar. The load heaved . . . Bill felt himself moving across.

Then 'What's happening?' he gasped as he felt the water suddenly rise to his knees. Was the water rising or was the cart sinking?

His panic-stricken glance ran along the horse's back. It was under water! Captain was swimming . . . Looking down, Bill could see the huge feet treading water and the bushy hair above Captain's hooves spreading like seaweed.

The cart, with its load of wool, was floating just below the surface of the rising tide. Bill glanced at the wheel immediately behind him. It was turning like a Mississippi paddle steamer, seaweed clinging to the spokes.

Mercifully the horse's head – which was thrust well out of the water – was leading the way to the far side.

Bill held on, praying as he'd never prayed before. What would he tell his father and the other farmers if he lost their wool? To say nothing of the horse and cart . . .

Suddenly the sweetest sound he had ever heard in his short life reached his ears – Captain's hooves scrambling to find a foothold, followed by a loud crunch as the huge wheels spun and caught on to the pebbly river bed.

Captain hauled himself and his load eagerly up the beach, with water pouring from the back of the cart, from the harness, Bill's clogs, his trousers. He jumped shakily from his perch on the shaft and vainly tried to squeeze the water from his trouser legs.

The horse shook himself in an equally vain attempt to rid himself of his dripping harness, his sides heaving with the effort of reaching safety.

*   *   *

'Ten minutes later and you would have wet more than your arse!' cackled an old chap who must have watched the whole of Bill's ordeal from the beach.

'What can you expect anyway from an inland farmer?' he said, tapping his walking stick on a name plate which proudly displayed his name and that of his farm.

'Never mind. You're not the first that's been caught crossing from Saltcoats,' he said more sympathetically when he saw Bill's crestfallen face. 'You'll be going to the station then, lad?'

'Aye, I thought I was taking a short cut. I'll know better the next time.'

Bill was thankful that the old man didn't recognise his father's name. At least, this tale had little chance of finding its way to Jackson's ears.

Apart from being soaked and a bit breathless, Captain seemed to have survived the crossing undamaged. With a bit of luck, the harness would dry before he reached home . . . As for himself, Bill knew his clothes would dry

16

on him – a bit of discomfort was a small price to pay if disaster had been averted.

His legs felt a bit weak as he led the dripping horse up the road towards the railway station.

'I reckon you must have got caught in the tide, judging by the state of these bottom bags,'' said the station master as he checked the wool in.

'Oh, my God!' gasped Bill, 'I bet they'll weigh twice as much now they're wet.'

'No, it's only the outside of the bags. I think they must have floated a bit.'

'Thank Heavens! It'll be bad enough when my father hears about this.'

'Why should he? Only you and me know about it, and I'm not going to say a word if he makes any enquiries about your journey. I've seen it happen to a good many others.' At last the day was turning out better. Bill took the longer route home, anxiously eyeing the wooden cart, the gear and his clothes as they slowly dried in the late summer sun.

'It's taken you long enough,' snapped his father as the weary horse and man halted near the stable door.

'I've finished milking, and your mother is anxious about you, so you'd better go on in for something to eat while I unsaddle him. I can't understand why your mother should worry about you when you've been riding around like the gentry all day . . . I've spent my time sharpening the binder knives ready to cut that big cornfield next week, *and* I've had to do all the milking.'

Bill jumped down from the cart and hurried inside the farmhouse, only turning at the doorway to give a backward glance at his father who was leading Captain towards the stable.

If that had been Peggy, she would have been telling him the entire story, he thought to himself as he made his way in the direction of the cooking smells.

'Aren't you and Len going to Bootle tonight?' Esther asked her brother as he sat down.

'Yes we are. I have plenty of time, he's not coming until half-past seven.'

* * *

'It was fine, I found the way to the station well enough,' Bill lied, replying to his friend's question.

This is the way to travel, he thought, as they bounced along the road.

When they sped past the Saltcoats turn-off he felt a cold shudder. That was certainly a road he didn't fancy taking again. Thank goodness his father didn't know about his disastrous crossing, and the chances of him hearing about it were remote. Bill could relax and enjoy his night out.

The hall looked bright and gay – the stage had been decorated with coloured strips of plastic. 'They've certainly gone to town with the trimmings,' laughed Len. 'It must have cost a small fortune to pay for all this plastic.'

'Well, it's a new thing and I must say they've done you proud. Let's hope the dance is up to their expectations and we get a good crowd,' said Bill. 'I'll sit here at the front where I can get a good view of things.'

The evening was a success and the band played well, as it always did with an appreciative audience.

During the interval the dancers and the band mingled and enjoyed the buffet.

'I always like playing in village halls,' said Len to the tall blonde he'd been watching in the first half. 'The only trouble is that it's hard to find time to have a dance!'

'Can't you make time? I like a quickstep. If the rest of them can manage on their own I'll save the next one for you.'

'Fine!' said Len, tucking into his third piece of cake.

He turned to Bill who was chatting to a small dark-haired girl. 'I saw you dancing with most of the prettiest girls in the room!' he chuckled.

'Well, I've had such a rotten day so far, I reckon I deserve a bit of fun before it ends!'

'What happened to you?' asked the pretty girl.

'It's too complicated to explain . . . and best forgotten!'

'There's the band leader making his way to the stage,' said Len. 'See you at the end, Bill. Hope you all enjoy the second half.'

'Well, I'm glad you asked me to come, Len. I haven't enjoyed such a good night out for ages . . . You lot in the band don't half know how to keep things moving!'

They were still laughing as the car sped along the road above the Ravenglass estuary. Bill glanced out of the car window. The harvest moon had cast a silvery cloak over the gleaming water, and the black shadowy outlines of the sand dunes were thrown into sharp relief, as though they had been painted on to the still surface of the sea. A calm and innocent scene . . . a seascape seemingly incapable of tempting, then trapping, and finally claiming as its own, any unwary man or beast who ventured across it!'

What a day this had been, thought Bill to himself, shivering slightly.

* * *

'Plastic decorations. . . Is that what you call that slippery, fancy stuff?' laughed Jackson the next morning when Bill described the fun they had had at the dance the night before.

'How much did it cost you to get into this *plastic* entertainment?'

'A shilling.'

'That's a dear do! You could have danced around the yard with a sweeping brush for nowt. . . But I reckon you had a very enjoyable day before that, even before you went to the dance! You weren't in need of any extra entertainment as far as I can see!'

Bill's blood froze! What did his father mean?

'What do you mean, Dad? Yesterday was a long hard one for me.'

He waited while his father refilled his mug of tea.

'You must have had plenty of time to spare yesterday when you reached Ravenglass, I reckon you spent an hour or so just sitting sunbathing on the beach – it's your mother's fault . . . '

'What's Mother's fault?' asked Esther, coming into the kitchen with some more hot water for the tea.

'A soon as there's a bit of sun she encourages you all to go to Seascale to spend a lazy afternoon on the beach. God knows why! The sun shines on you just as well if you're working in the fields. Sunbathing is for the rich and idle, and there's plenty of them at Seascale.'

'What makes you so sure I had time to waste sitting on the beach, Dad?' Bill said uneasily.

Well, if you *didn't* take Captain's saddle off while you laid about in the sun, can you explain to me why I found a big lump of seaweed stuck under it when I unharnessed him last night? I suppose you just threw it down while you enjoyed yourself, then didn't check it properly when you put it back on the poor horse.'

Bill, flabbergasted, just nodded in agreement!

2

SHOW DAY

'Thank God it's a fine morning, Bill,' observed Jackson as they crossed the yard to do the milking.

'You mean for the show, Dad?'

'What else do you think I'm talking about on the first Friday in September? It's been a show day for as long as I can remember. You ask such daft questions. I can't think of anything else to look forward to at this time of the year.'

'It's getting near our Esther's birthday – you could have been thinking about that,' laughed Bill, knowing his father's total disregard for such occasions.

'Oh is it? How old is she then? Let's see, she must be nearing eleven or so.'

'More like thirteen, Dad.'

'Thirteen! Do you mean to tell me that I've kept her till that age and she's not working yet? Good God! When I was her age I'd been working for, let me see . . . a couple of years or so. We left school in those days when we'd learnt to read, could count a bit, and somebody was willing to take us on. School can only do so much for a chap, then he has to make his own way in the world. Besides, one or two of us grew a bit too big for them little desks they had in Bookwell School. I think the teacher was glad when we cleared off and made room for the little kids.'

'That takes an awful lot of believing, Dad. What about the Attendance Officer?'

'Never heard of such a chap – what does he do?'

'Looks for pupils playing truant and takes them back to school.'

Jackson laughed loudly at the thought. 'He would have had to make his way up to Wasdale Head then, which

21

would have taken him a good bit out of his way, and it would have been pointless. The likes of us had no need of an education. Them Herdwicks can't read, and that's what I spent my days with. Folk who lived in Egremont had to be able to read. And they had to count well too, in case they came across dishonest folk who were well enough educated to cheat them. No, lad. So long as you know enough to get by, that's all that's needed.'

'But haven't you had to be able to read and write well – as a farmer?'

'Your mother sees to all that for me. Good sense in choosing a wife is another important thing for a young man?'

'I'll choose a wife because I think she's pretty. I won't set her a test to see if she's cleverer than me!'

'To think I let you go to school until you wore the same size clothes as me just to hear you say a bloody daft thing like that.'

'What do you mean, Dad?'

'I couldn't have set your mother, or anybody else, a test, let alone know whether they'd got the answers right or wrong. All you have to do is look and see what the lass wears most days. It's simple as that . . . And shove that bloody cat out of the way or you'll put your clog on it and we'll have a murder on our hands. The poor little bugger's been waiting for its breakfast for the last hour. Unlike you, with all your education, it knows fine well you're late for milking again . . . and it can't even read the bloody clock!'

Bill settled himself to milk the nearest cow. Waiting until he could hear the steady stream of milk striking the nearside of the empty bucket between his father's legs, he pursued his line of questioning. 'What did you mean when you said you could choose a suitable wife by the way she was dressed?'

'You don't listen properly, Bill,' Jackson snarled. 'I never said anything about *how* a woman dressed, but what she wore *most* days.'

'I don't follow you.'

The sound of the milk was now almost inaudible as it rained into the froth without striking the sides of Jackson's pail; the level of the milk had risen rapidly as the powerful hands drew a steady unhesitating stream from the cow's udder.

Jackson shuffled slightly without changing tempo, and spat a brown stream of tobacco juice expertly into the channel below his cow's feet, before continuing . . . 'Well, lad, it's like this. . . A thrifty woman will wear the same dress for a long time, she'll keep it clean, she won't be turning up in something different every time you see her. But a woman who's costing her father a pretty penny will be just as bad or worse when it comes to digging in her husband's pocket.'

'What if you fall in love with a woman? It would be hard not to marry her whatever she wears?'

'Well, I suppose you'll be like most of us – you'll marry a lass who takes your eye. But a wise word in your ear might help you to look the other way if you spot a real extravagant one. After all, an ugly wife is very ready to be trained. She's so pleased at catching a reasonable chap that she's glad to stop at home and behave herself. You know, lad, I remember a young farmer who lived way up beyond Gosforth. He bought a motorbike, then travelled as far as Whitehaven to the north and Millom to the south to the dances. Likely, he was looking for something a bit smarter than anything they could breed in the Gosforth area.'

Jackson eased himself up painfully from the cow he had milked, his pail brimming with warm, frothy milk. Then he made his way to the byre door. 'It's taking you long enough to finish that heifer,' he said. 'I'm expecting you to get those calves washed and shampooed up for the show today. The rate you're going, you'll have to enter them for the last hound trail of the afternoon because that's all that'll be left of the entertainment.'

Bill cursed under his breath. He knew he couldn't milk

as fast as his father, even when he'd been left the easy milker.

'Did the chap from Gosforth find a wife then?' he asked as they both settled down to milk another couple of cows.

'Oh, aye, he did – one from Millom. That's why I got a bit bothered when you went down that way dancing the other week.'

'What's wrong with Millom? I noticed some nice-looking lasses down there. After all, it's not at the far end of the world, Dad.'

'That just depends what sort of travelling you do. Those of us who work for a living on a farm can't spare the time to traipse about with womenfolk when they want to go as far as Millom or maybe Cockermouth to ask their mother how to bake a pie-crust or to see if one of their relatives is getting better from the flu.'

'What about the chap from Gosforth then?' asked the exasperated Bill.

'I'm glad you asked me that . . . He soon discovered that his wife was worse than a Herdwick to pen up! The poor chap would land back from Whitehaven auction many a Thursday expecting a hot meal . . . expecting her to have milked the few cows they had, to have fed the calves and the pigs and watered the bull . . . Jobs every farmer's wife should be able to manage while her man does a bit of essential buying and selling on a Thursday.'

'And a bit of gossiping and drinking to boot!' Bill thought to himself.

'But like as not, continued Jackson, there wouldn't be a single light in the windows as he stepped out of Eli Tyson's car at his road end. Off she'd gone to catch the Millom bus as soon as he'd left that morning, gone to see her mother . . . The stock would be bawling their hungry heads off.'

'When did she come back home?'

'Usually at the weekend, if he was lucky.'

'How did it all end?'

'Divorce! It was the scandal of the district. Usually it's

only the rich who can afford the luxury of changing a wife, but I expect an ordinary chap can also reach the end of his tether. It doesn't happen very often in these country spots. Most of us have a bit more of an idea of what we want when we look for a wife.'

'It sounds a bit like buying a good horse. You check to see if she's sound in wind and limb, with a good staying record!'

'Now you've got the idea exactly. Maybe my words will be of some help when you're gadding about the dance halls and such spots. Look and see how often she wears the same dress . . . It's as good a guide to choosing a wife as anything you can read in them fancy magazines I see lying around our house. What was I reading the other day? Advice pages or some such thing?'

'That was a women's magazine you were looking at. Those articles are written to advise young women about choosing a husband.'

'What a daft idea! All a woman has to do is clap her eye on a chap who can afford to keep her and who doesn't live too far from her mother's house. They get their money for nothing some of these folk. It's just like all them farming magazines – always keen to tell us working farmers how to spend our money on fancy drugs and expensive machinery. I expect common sense ideas won't sell a magazine.'

'So why are you in such a big hurry to get to the show this morning, Dad? I'm sure you'll visit the agricultural stands, even though they're all trying to sell you the latest in farming equipment!'

'Yes, lad, I'll pay a visit to every one of them. I like to see what's in the forefront in the agricultural world, but that doesn't mean I'll be daft enough to buy anything. No, I'm too wise an old bird for that! I'll just take a walk round so that if I'm ever asked a question about modern farming I'll be able to answer intelligently. There's no sense in not being up-to-date, that would just make me an ignorant old man . . . and besides I like reckoning up how much I can save by hanging on to my old machinery. I did old friends a favour by buying most of it at their farm sales and when a thing has worked well for them I reckon it could be as useful for me.'

'You'll never have anything up-to-date if you always buy somebody else's cast-offs, Dad.'

'Once I bought a brand-new corn seed drill – a lovely painted machine it was. Peggy didn't know what she was pulling behind her when we set off up yon field by the road. Folk from all over the district stopped to have a look at it. I think it was the paint that caught everybody's eye – bright yellow and red – you could spot it a good mile off.'

'What was wrong with it?'

'Nothing. The machine was faultless. Up and down the field we went; the seed corn flowed through the pipes a treat. We worked all day Peggy and me . . . and at the end we were both buggered. Then we took the rattling thing back home. What a grand noise it made. But it sowed the corn fine.'

'So why haven't we got it now? If it was new in your lifetime we should still have it – we have everybody else's heirlooms!'

'Well, lad, the corn grew up fine, but in straight lines. It didn't look natural-like. You could see the long empty lines where the wheels had gone up and down. It was lucky I'd sown it straight or the whole neighbourhood would have said I'd been drunk.'

'So what did you do the following year?'

'I looked at the drill and thought about all the trouble trundling that noisy bit of apparatus down the road was, letting everybody hear what I was up to. And, in addition, I'd had to take another horse and cart to carry the seed corn in! So I decided Peggy and me would make one quiet journey with the seed corn. She could be unsaddled and spend the day grazing the dyke-backs, while I walked up and down the field on my own scattering it by hand . . . as I've always done. That way I could be sure how thinly or thickly I was sowing it. You get a 'feel' for how much is just right, and that drill could have spoilt the yield if one of its pipes had hit a cobble and broken. So the next daft chap who took a fancy to it bought it at a reasonable price.'

'Who bought it then?'

'Alan Harrison. He always fancied himself as an up-to-date farmer. He was in one of them Young Farmers' Clubs even before he left school, a sure sign that he was ready to be blinded by a little bit of salesmanship.'

Bill laughed. 'You know, I've seen that drill many a springtime. He gets plenty of use out of it. I wonder what it's like working with such a good piece of machinery!'

'Just you watch when he turns into the wind and all that dust from the horse's feet, the wheels and them rattling pipes flies into his face. Then come and watch me throwing a few handfuls of corn where the only dry soil is blowing from my own clog bottoms – and ask yourself how comfortable a modern seed drill is.'

'All I can say is, I'm glad you're my dad and not someone I might have to buy or sell something to.'

'At the speed you're milking that cow you'll be lucky to make this week's wages!' retorted Jackson. 'I've got to sell the stuff before I get the money to pay the likes of you, so get a move on or we'll never get to the show ground with them two calves. I blame that Young Farmers' Club. Showing stock was always the pastime of the big farmers who had nothing better to amuse themselves with while their farm men did the hard work. Now you youngsters think we should show our stock off to the whole of West Cumberland . . . Most folk who go to the shows haven't any idea what makes a good animal anyway.'

'It doesn't matter. People from the towns and villages like to have a day out, and it's nice to meet people you haven't seen for years . . . You always manage to arrive home late with a good idea of who was in the beer tent!'

'That's where you get the best crack, lad. Them that spend the day brushing their bull's coat or polishing harness don't know how to enjoy themselves – they've usually spent the last 364 days planning for this one. No, no, I prefer my stock to live their lives a bit mucky, with badly shaped horns and a calm attitude to life, rather than be 'fought to death' with brushes, shampoo and ribbons.

The byre door opened and Esther appeared. 'Are you two still milking? I've been busy for the last two hours getting our two calves ready for the show!'

'I hope they're ready,' said her brother.

'Yes, Bill. They know something exciting is going to happen – they sense things.'

'I hope the shock doesn't slow their growth down,' grumbled Jackson. 'Hundreds of hands poking, patting and stroking them will be a new experience, as well as loudspeakers and light horses jumping over fences . . . They've never seen anything as daft as that. I just hope they don't get any ideas about jumping out of the field when they come home; they'll have seen so many strange things at the show, there'll be no coping with them for a while.'

'Don't talk silly, Dad. I've been practising leading them round on those pretty little halters for weeks and they're very well behaved now.'

'New halters! When will the expense end? I expect you to win a prize to help pay for all this extravagance.'

*   *   *

Jackson heard the noise of the preparations long before he reached the show field.

Startled animals bleated, whinnied, lowed and complained to each other across the field, whilst buckets rattled and farm machinery groaned and clanked into the required position. His gaze swept the field as the tents, flags and lorries came into view. He walked through the entrance and his eye rested, as usual, on the single line of misshapen trees which had bordered the far end of this

field for as long as he could remember. At least one pony
was tied to each tree. They were all colours and all sizes,
but a struggling farmer couldn't afford such luxuries.
Unless an animal could earn its keep it was of no use. Each
of his children in turn had begged for a riding pony but
such things were for those who had money to spare or
who had use for a light pony – for a milk trap or other light
carting work. Nevertheless Jackson liked the ponies and
cast his eye expertly over what was for sale.

'Can I interest you in one of my ponies this year,
Jackson? You have a close look every year, but never
actually buy one. Maybe this year you'll be tempted to
take the plunge?'

'Good day to you, Matt. I thought you wouldn't be very
far away from anybody with a keen eye and a bit of money
in his pocket this fine morning.'

'Just look at this bonny little skewbald . . . young, with

years of riding and light carting in her. I've only just finished breaking her in.'

'Who wants a nuisance of a Shetland? demanded Jackson. They're more trouble than a nagging, straying wife. A chap never knows what sort of mood it's going to waken up in! They talk about 'stupid as a mule' but these little buggers take a lot of beating for sheer cussedness! Besides, I've no harness to fit something as small as that.'

'She'd make a fine riding pony for your daughters.'

'Shetlands are too near the ground for riding on, and they have a few nasty ways of getting rid of their riders. No thanks, Matt. You've had a good try again this year . . . but save your breath for a customer who's easily taken in by a cute-looking pony.'

Jackson chuckled to himself as he walked away. He and Matt enjoyed their yearly no-sale transaction. Matt was a tinker by trade and followed all the shows and fairs . . . on the look-out for an easy pound or two.

The heavy horses always attracted Jackson – fine, well-groomed Clydesdales, with their ribbons and plaited tails catching the warm sunlight. It was hard to believe that these gleaming animals were ordinary working horses who had been sweating and hauling loads of hay and corn the day before. Their polished white and bluish mottled feet had splashed through mud, becks, cow muck; had rattled on the hot metalled roads. Now their coats had been brushed and brushed by eager loving hands to remove any traces of saddles, collars and harness.

Jackson ran his hands over their backs – they were sweet and clean, with no trace of sagging. He wondered at the resilience of these massive animals whose spines could accept such heavy weights day in and day out, earning their living proudly for so many years before eventually drooping exhausted and being relegated to light work.

His gaze travelled to the other side of the show ring where gleaming tractors, binders and those new-fangled balers were being manouevred into position. Young men were already gathering to inspect these modern giants which they hoped would make their daily work easier and quicker. Time must be saved. 'What for?' Jackson asked himself. 'What would you do with a machine once it was worn out? Could you ease it into light jobs? Could it reproduce itself at as little cost as a horse? Could you have a quiet crack with it like he often had with Peggy?'

Everything was bound to change. He wondered what an agricultural show would be like in fifty years' time. Would there be any horses like these?

Maybe Matt would be the winner in the end. Riding horses and ponies would always be in demand. Plenty of folk would be willing to buy a pony for their child, even if they had little idea of how to look after one. Horses need a lot of work. They have to be ridden every day if possible, that is if they're to be happy and healthy. A world that's geared to the lazy wouldn't be suitable for kids who fancy a pony one day, and something else the next. He shook his head. People from the towns already bought pups and then left them to roam the highways and byways . . . He hoped the time wouldn't come when ponies were left unattended, unloved . . . like forgotten ornaments . . . to decorate a field.

'You're looking very thoughtful today, Jackson.'

'Hello Tom! I'm just trying to see into the future. These horses are our bread and butter. What happens when them gleaming great tractors take over the farms? Who'll breed the horses then?'

'That's a good bit off yet, but you just have to look at the interest the young farmers are showing over there and you can see the way it's going to be. More leisure time would be a great thing for us, instead of working from dawn till dusk.'

'Well, I'm going to have a look at the milk cows. At least no one's invented a machine that can change grass into milk yet, nor can they make artificial meat and wool.'

'Just give them time' thought Tom to himself as he followed Jackson towards the rows of pristine cows.

* * *

'You're late tonight, Jackson?' observed Jean from behind the bar at the Grey Mare.

'I've had a great day at the show. I wasn't sure I'd make it tonight. A chap can only do so much in one day.'

'You mean you can only drink so much in one day,' she laughed as she pulled the farmer's pint.

'The trouble with you publicans is that you only worry about the money we might be spending elsewhere.'

'I bet she's not wrong about you visiting the beer tent,' laughed John Steel.

'An hour in the beer tent is a grand idea,' pronounced Jackson. 'I met a good few friends who I wouldn't have seen if I'd just wandered about telling folk what dab hands they are at breeding stock.'

Jackson was very genial after his enjoyable day, and his reminiscences kept the conversation going until late. But tiredness eventually reminded him that it was time to head home.

'I noticed our Esther won third prize with that heifer of hers . . . so I'll have to get back and say something to please her,' he announced at long last.

'She's done well,' nodded Jean from the busy bar.

'That's what *she'll* be thinking . . . She'll be very pleased with herself. Little does she realise that shampooing a cow's tail to catch the judge's eye is one thing but good breeding is a lifetime's occupation.'

'Get yourself out of here, Jackson,' Jean snapped in exasperation, 'while I still have enough patience to talk politely to you. You've been carried away by your own story-telling to the point where you can't tell fact from fiction. You don't give the lass a good word.'

'Well *I'm* the one who's got to live with her when the show's over!' protested Jackson, getting up to leave.

3

THE DUN-COLOURED SHIRE

'Bill's a long time coming for his breakfast this morning. What on earth can he be doing?' wondered Edith.

'He's gone to catch a couple of horses,' replied Jackson. 'We need to start early this morning. The weather's good and we have a lot of ploughing to finish off today. That is, if he gets himself back here before dinnertime.'

'I think I can hear him coming in now. A good thing too – his breakfast won't keep much longer.'

Bill hurried into the farm kitchen, a worried look on his face.

'What's the matter Bill?' asked his mother anxiously.

'I can't find Captain! He's not in the field, I've looked everywhere.'

'Don't be so bloody daft, lad,' said Jackson. 'How can a big Shire get lost? He stands higher than most of the hedges around here. Now if you couldn't find a few Herdwicks or a couple of Shetland ponies then I would have said the little buggers had got out of the field. But a great big, home-loving gelding like Captain wouldn't know how to get lost. I expect I'll have to go and fetch him in myself. It's a right state of affairs when a chap's got to do every little job himself, just because an idle son can't find a bloody horse that stands nigh on the height of an elephant.'

'I've looked everywhere, Dad,' insisted Bill. 'I've even been over to Tom's farm to see if Captain wandered into one of his fields during the night.'

'You've been to tell the neighbours that we can't keep our stock in – they won't know when to stop laughing in the pub next time I decide to have a pint! What made you go to Tom's? Was there a gate left open?'

'No.'

'Well, how the hell could he have got out? I've never taught him how to open gates. And he's too keen on his grub to bother jumping over the dyke. Sit down and eat your breakfast while I go and catch the bloody thing myself.'

'I knew he'd have plenty to say Mam, but I looked everywhere . . . Like he says, it's pretty hard to lose a good-natured horse like Captain.'

'Especially if there was no gate open,' agreed Edith. 'Are you sure he hasn't wandered back into the stable? The field is next to the farm buildings and he might have thought he had some food left in his trough.'

'I looked. The mares and their foals were still in the field. If only they could talk, they could tell us where he was.'

'It's no good wishing that. There must be an explanation. You haven't looked thoroughly enough . . . A horse can't just vanish into thin air.'

'You sound like Dad. As sure as shot, he'll march in through the gate with Captain trailing at his heels as large as life.'

* * *

Half an hour later the sound of hurrying clogs reached their ears, accompanied by a rising tide of expletives.

'My God what's wrong,' moaned Bill. 'Do I stay put, and face his temper, or disappear for an hour or two? He's obviously found Captain.'

'No, I haven't heard Captain's feet on the cobbles,' said Edith. 'There must be something amiss.'

'Amiss! Amiss!' stormed Jackson, hurrying into the kitchen. 'It's more than just "amiss" . . . The bloody stupid thing's fallen into the septic tank! He must have decided to walk across the lids and the last one gave way.'

'Is he still alive or has he drowned?' asked Edith.

'He's alive, only his head is sticking out above the liquid
. . . If we didn't have two mares newly foaled I'd have left
the daft bugger where he is. It's going to take us some time
and effort to pull him out. A Clydesdale wouldn't have
been heavy enough to fall through them thick lids . . .
These Shires are nowt but a bloody nuisance. The only
thing to be said in his favour is that he was big enough to
reach the bottom and keep his head above water.'

'Poor thing, he must be frightened. No wonder Bill
couldn't find him. You know, Jackson, I've told you the
septic tank was dangerous. You should have fenced it in
and put a warning notice up – it's too near the house.'

'I can't see that a notice would have made any difference. I haven't found time to teach the stock to read any
more than I've found time to teach them to shut gates! I
knew he must be in the field somewhere. And sure
enough, there he was, trying to reach a few blades of grass
at the edge of the tank. He'll take some getting out – we'll
have to rope him, Bill. You'd better go back to Tom's and
see if one or two of his men'll come and give us a hand. It'll
be like pulling a ton of slippery fish out of that mess. And
seeing as you've told the entire neighbourhood that
something's "amiss", we might as well give them the
whole story to talk about.'

Raising a heavy horse without the benefit of lifting gear
was a daunting task and it was an hour or so before the
huge animal was standing shivering at the side of the pit.
The other horses and their foals had been moved to
another field, their curiosity making them too much of a
nuisance for the working men.

'For goodnes sake Bill, get the bloody thing hosed down
before anybody else sees it. I don't want passers-by to have
to guess what colour it was yesterday. Thank God it's a
black Shire. A light grey would have shown the stains for a
good few weeks.'

'It's enough to give the poor animal pneumonia,' said

Edith, as they were eating their tea before milking time. 'And you took him ploughing this afternoon, Jackson.'

'What are you complaining about? *He* doesn't know he nearly drowned in a tank of shit! All he knew this afternoon was that he had to snort and cough to clear his nostrils of the stench. A bit of exercise soon cleared his breathing passages. I was doing him a favour. Mind you, I got a bit of a face full every time we turned back into the wind. There was no way I could escape the fumes. If Bill had washed him down a bit better it would have made it a more comfortable afternoon's work for me.'

'I washed him as best I could, but *you* try cleaning his mane and tail when you don't stand as high as him.'

'It all comes of having water closets fitted,' asserted his father. 'If we'd stuck to dry closets there wouldn't be any traps to catch unsuspecting stock in. Closets inside houses aren't very clean anyway. They even have water closets *inside* schools these days. It must make a school an awful smelly place to be! When I was a youngster we had to go across the yard to a reasonable distance from the main building. Now that's what I call hygienic . . . Is that the right word, Jane?'

'Yes, Dad, it is. But it is cleaner to have water closets – who wants to walk across a yard in the rain?'

'I expect the lads that smoke can be caught easier as well. Indoor closets must make the entire building stink.

'They shouldn't be smoking in the first place,' retorted an indignant Edith.

'You're like all women, Edith. You think you can change the world just by saying a thing is wrong. When will you good people realise that the more you forbid youngsters to do a thing the more determined they'll be to have a go? It's like putting up notices to warn folk that there's a cesspit under their feet . . . They'll just walk over the lid to see if the notice is telling the truth. Human nature is always contrary.'

'It's not the only thing that's contrary,' muttered Bill to himself.

*   *   *

The Grey Mare was noisy, with the pump working at double speed to satisfy the thirsty clients, spring being a very busy time on the farms.

'There's been an awful lot of ploughing, harrowing and tatie setting done over the last week or two in this district,' laughed Tom Graham as he downed yet another pint.

'No wonder this place is full. I reckon we've all earned a drink or two,' agreed John Steel. 'But no one has earned his drink more than Jackson Strong.'

'Why? What has he done, John?'

'He seems to have either bred . . . or bought . . . a new strain of Shire horse.'

'How do you make that out then?'

'I was working in that twelve-acre of mine when I happened to look up and there was Jackson with the strangest-looking Shire I've ever seen.'

At his words Jackson looked up from his game of dominoes. 'What did you see in my field, John? For a chap who had twelve acres to harrow before tea it's strange that you had time to gaze about at other folk who were earning a decent living by minding their own business in their own fields. I didn't come into this pub to make any sort of comment on the two weary Clydesdales you were persuading to pull a set of harrows that our Peggy could have pulled on her own, even though she's just dropped a foal.'

'Go on with what you were saying, John,' urged Joe Watson, curious to know what lay behind the remark.

'Well, Jackson has a black Shire, as you may well know. And, as most folk here know, Shires come as either light grey or black . . . The fact that he was working a dun-coloured one alongside Peggy this morning was a bit of a surprise. I know he likes to breed unusual stock, but I've spent all day trying to work out how he managed to arrive at a yellowish-brown Shire. You *could* make a mix of sorts with one or two different breeds, but to get a smooth finish on its coat like that takes a bit of doing.'

Some of the farmers in the pub had already heard about Jackson's escapade with the cesspit and were having a quiet chuckle as they waited for the farmer's response.

'You folk have very short memories,' he declared equably, as though addressing a rather slow group of infants.' It wasn't so long ago that the government was asking us to do all sorts of things for the war effort.'

'The war effort was years ago, Jackson. What far-fetched tale are you thinking up now?'

'The truth is John, . . . that none of us knew how long the war was going to last and, as it turned out, one of my ideas for the war effort didn't materialise until last week.'

'Oh come on, tell us a better one than that.'

'Just give me a minute and I'll explain. . .Maybe a pint'll jog my memory a bit. . .Thanks Tom! If you all think back to the beginning of the war, Churchill and his advisers sent all sorts of information leaflets out to us ignorant farmers, advising us to keep our farms in darkness in case "Gerry" spotted us and decided to drop bombs, thinking we were an important factory or something. . .And you may also remember that they suggested we should use camouflage during daylight hours so that they couldn't see white cows and horses easily.'

'What has that got to do with your horse?'

'Don't you see? The best way of camouflaging an animal is to make it change its colour . . . preferably to khaki, like the army. So I got the idea of breeding khaki horses. But you can't do something like that in five minutes, or even in ten years. So, for once, my breeding schedule took longer than I had bargained for, and the war was over before my new anti-aircraft horse was perfected.'

Jackson reached for his waiting pint as a murmur of disbelief ran round the pub. He glanced in the direction of a group of young people from the town who had listened closely to his explanation, not knowing if the tale was true or not.

'Now you youngsters,' he said addressing them more directly, 'have no way of knowing whether I'm speaking the truth or no – I can see that by your faces. Well, all I have to say is that the last war was won by people with imagination and good ideas . . . If I recall correctly, there was an attack on a dam somewhere in Germany that used the idea of a flat round stone bouncing along and skimming the surface of the lake instead of sinking. Now that same thing is quite a common pastime for country folk, so us farmers are pretty god at thinking up ways and means of solving any problems that worry the likes of Churchill . . . The only problem was that I didn't get the breeding pattern finished before the end of the war.'

'Never mind, Jackson. When the next war starts we'll all send a letter to the government volunteering you as a technical adviser to the war office!' retorted John, laughing at the ingenious way the old man had tried to talk himself out of an embarrassing situation.

'Would that mean I could have one of those "by appointment" signs put up over my byre door?'

John laughed. 'No such luck, Jackson. You'd have to sell milk or beef to the Queen for that.'

'I don't reckon she needs any of our produce. I've seen photos in the *Farmers' Weekly* of her private farms with some prize-winning cattle and horses . . . They do well enough without any contribution from us . . . and in the same article it said that she has a keen eye for a well-bred horse.'

'That's true enough, Jackson,' agreed John.

'But,' finished Jackson proudly, 'I don't reckon she'll own a horse that's exactly the same shade of dun as my Captain!'

4

FIRESIDE TALES

Edith glanced out of the window anxiously.

'I invited Tom and Mary to come across for a cup of tea and a bite to eat tonight, Jackson, but it looks as though it's about to snow.'

'It's taken you a long time to notice. It's been threatening to snow all day.'

'Well I haven't your nose for bad weather, Jackson . . .'

'No, you've got to see it falling out of the heavens before you have any idea what's happening. It's a good thing us farmers can read the skies or we'd be caught out in the rain many a time. But I'm pleased you've invited Tom over. It'll be a welcome change from some of the folk you invite.'

'If you mean our May, then you must remember, Jackson, that I can't choose my relatives any more than you can.'

'It's not just May . . . Why we've got to entertain folk like the vicar I don't know . . . As though May wasn't sanctimonious enough!'

'He seemed a very nice chap from what Mam said about him,' volunteered Esther.

'You'll have to learn that a chap isn't all he appears to be,' snapped her father.'

Esther chuckled to herself. 'I have a good notion about men. We've a couple in this house who take quite a lot of understanding!'

'Here's Mary now,' exclaimed Edith. 'But I can't see Tom . . .'

'He'll be finishing his work, like as not. A chap can't stroll round the countryside as though he has nowt to do.'

'You mean he doesn't want to be seen walking with his wife . . . in case you ignorant farmers talk about him taking his wife for a walk like a town chap does,' laughed Esther. 'You're all alike. I've never seen a farmer walking beside his wife in my life. Even when Jack was a baby Mary pushed the pram here by the road while Tom walked the short way across the fields!'

'That's right, Esther,' agreeed her mother. 'Some men take more training than others!'

'If a chap's busy you women read all sorts of nonsense into what he does . . . Come in and have a seat Mary.' Jackson said thankfully, welcoming their visitor. 'Tom won't be far behind?'

'You don't think he'd want to be seen walking with me, do you Jackson? He'll arrive in another few minutes . . . But I'm certainly glad to be in the warmth. It's just starting to snow.'

Soon Tom arrived and the group was seated around the warm fire enjoying the farmhouse tea and cakes.

'It's a grand thing to sit here and enjoy a tea like this, Edith,' said Tom. 'We should all be thankful that times are better now.'

'It's hard to believe you were all so badly off that you couldn't afford to have a decent tea!' laughed Esther.

'I was brought up in a little village not far from Ravenglass and there used to be plenty of poverty in spite of the rich men's houses nearby. Most of us who went to the village school were poor. Like a lot of the other kids, I had to walk a long way to school every morning and had to carry a few sandwiches to eat at dinnertime. One day the schoolmaster asked us all what we had brought to eat. "Bread and jam, Sir" answered a few . . . "Bread and cheese, Sir" said one or two more . . . "Dry bread, Sir," answered one of the really poor ones. Then the master asked Tim, whose father was a gamekeeper, what his mother had put in his sandwiches. Tim answered truthfully, "Cold pheasant, Sir". . .The master was so angry at the lad pretending to be better than the others that he gave him a good clout round the ears for telling lies!'

'That's a disgrace! Teachers should have more sense and make sure they're right before they do a thing like that,' protested Esther.

'Possibly,' Tom answered. 'But teachers aren't always thinkers. They expect kids to make mistakes. They don't want to spend time checking the truth. In any case a good clout is a healthy thing for youngsters – it keeps them awake and paying attention.'

'Truth is often stranger than fiction,' Edith nodded sagely. 'Folk forget that what's a luxury for some is everyday food for others. . . I should think the same lad would hardly know what a good piece of beef was.'

'Talking about pheasants and birds reminds me of the time I went to Grasmere. . .'

'You won't know anybody from Grasmere, Jackson. Come on, tell us another one!'

'I can see you don't have any idea of geography, Tom. You think Grasmere is a good distance from here. Well, so it is if you go round by the road. But if you had lived up Wasdale Head like I used to, then you would have had to cross the fells to get anywhere over on that side of the county. You see, it was like this. . .'

Jackson reached for another slice of cake, then looked round the ring of expectant faces.

'It was a bit of a slack time up the valley and la'al Jimmy Marshall, who worked on the same farm as me and was from Grasmere, fancied going home to see his family. Old Clem, our boss, looked at us for a long time when we asked if we could both go. He knocked his pipe out against the grate, then made his decision. ''Yes, lads, you can have a couple of days off to go and see your folks. But don't get lost in the fells – I won't bother to come and look for you. Lads are easy come by, so I'll keep your jobs for a few days. . . After that I'll reckon you've got lost – or found something better.'' '

'Didn't he care about your safety?' asked a shocked Esther.

'Why should he? If we were daft enough to trail off into them lonely hills then it was our own lookout. After all, he cared as much about us as we cared about him!'

Jackson paused while Edith refilled his mug. He liked to keep his listeners waiting.

'So, early the next morning we set off. It was about three o'clock, earlier than we ever thought about getting out of bed for work. Thank God there were only a couple of milking cows on the farm that the boss could manage to milk himself. Mind you, I had second thoughts after we had struggled up to the top of Sty Head Pass. My best boots were heavy and I had a hole in one sock which rubbed like the very devil! Anyhow when we reached the top we stopped, turned, and looked down on Wasdale valley lying far below.

"That's the last time I'll ever see that sight," said la'al Jimmy.

"What do you mean?" I asked.

"Well, I have no intention of going back to work for yon bugger. I was born in Grasmere, and when my father died I wanted to work in the slate quarries where there was good money to be made, but my mother reckoned it would be better if I worked on a farm until I was a bit bigger and stronger. She didn't reckon on that hungry kitchen down there, so I'm off back home. Just think on that you remember the road back here. That is if you really want to stay buried in that bloody farm." '

'Didn't you think of turning back, Jackson?' asked Mary, intrigued.

'Not on your life! A few days holiday was something I'd never had before ... and in any case I was young and wasn't in the habit of thinking about what might happen the day after tomorrow, so finding the way back could look after itself. It was a beautiful morning in July. What could be finer than a taste of freedom and an unknown track ahead?'

'Go on then, let's hear what happened next,' urged Bill, who'd lowered his paper to listen to the tale.

'Another slice of that gingerbread would help me remember a lot better. It's hard thinking back forty years or more.'

Cake and more tea were handed round by the two women, enabling the old farmer to continue his train of thought. 'It was a lot longer walk than I expected. Jimmy reckoned it was only over the top of Sty Head, downhill to Dungeon Ghyll, through by Chapel Stile, and then he would be nearly home,' said Jackson as he attacked his gingerbread. 'Them dalesmen don't have any notion of distance. They don't count walking downhill; they reckon mileage only in uphill drag and everything else as a bonus. I suppose Jimmy was like our workhorses. . . As soon as his nose was pointing homewards he didn't think owt about the hours of walking.'

Jackson paused as his mind travelled back. 'When I come to think of it, it was a great walk. The scenery was a grand sight, if that's what you like. Although it beats me why so many folk come away up here from their comfortable town houses to spend hours in the rain and cold just looking at wet slippery rocks. I mean, I was doing somebody a favour keeping them company on their way home. I wasn't just wandering about trying to get lost, like a good many of the visitors do these days.'

'They don't get lost on purpose,' laughed Edith. 'They often have problems with the maps and lack of signposts, I suppose.'

'Jimmy didn't need any map. He just knew the way from what he'd been told at home.'

'It beats me why he needed you to keep him company,' mused Tom. 'I'm sure he'd have made a lot faster time on his own. After all, I don't reckon you were ever a lish young chap.'

'That's just where you're wrong, Tom. I was never what you'd call skinny and wiry, with a neck like a turkey cock,

46

like them Lake District chaps. But I was lish and full of fettle. Besides, I learned a lot more about Jimmy as we went along. I was only a young chap at the time but I soon learnt how superstitious them dalesmen are.'

'What on earth do you mean?' asked Mary. 'I've always thought the miners and farmers around here were the most superstitious folk you could find.'

'That's because you've never travelled further than your own doorstep,' replied Jackson. 'You women don't have any curiosity about what might be going on outside your own area. I suppose it's because you're ruled by mealtimes and never have to organise anything more complicated.'

'You can put it that way if you like, but wasting hours trying to get lost in the hills isn't my idea of how to spend my spare time,' Mary retorted.

'Well, I learnt a lot from the few days I spent with Jimmy, believe me.'

'What did you mean when you said the lad was superstitious?' asked Esther.

'That's the whole reason why he asked me to go with him. You see, we were just finding our way down a spot called . . . Let me see, now what was it called?'

He paused, searching for the name.

'It was something like . . . Russet Gill. At least, I know it was a gill, but the name sounded a bit like a sort of apple. Russet Gill, I reckon it was. No sign of any apple trees, mind you. Just a stony path, crags and a noisy beck. I noticed that Jimmy was glancing around and looking a bit uneasy. I asked him if he'd lost his way. I mean to say, we could have been coming down into any valley in the district for all I knew. I was beginning to feel a bit uneasy myself. "Oh no, I haven't missed the way," he said. . . "I'm just taking care that we pass the grave without disturbing the ghost."

"What ghost?" I asked.'

A titter rippled around the fireplace.

'I knew we would hear some outlandish story if we sat here long enough,' laughed Bill sceptically.

'If you don't believe it, just come to Gosforth Show with me next year and have a crack with Jimmy. He comes this far every year to see what we're up to on this side of the county. . . The trouble with you folk is that you only stray as far as Whitehaven Auction and back – that's a sure way of bypassing interesting ways of life further afield.'

'Go on, Dad. Tell us about the ghost,' urged an enthralled Esther.

Her father continued. 'Sure enough, as we made our way down this path, the beck seemed to get noisier and noisier, while Jimmy got more and more nervous. . . An uncanny silence pressed down on us, like a heavy hand reaching down from the summits which towered above our path.'

Jackson paused, then continued, his voice rising slightly. 'Suddenly Jimmy left the path and made his way to what looked like a heap of stones. I followed, and as I got closer I saw that the stones had been placed in the shape of a cross. . . Jimmy was muttering a few prayers when I reached him. I didn't dare speak until we had both moved back and were once again descending the path. "Most folk say a prayer there," said Jimmy, "just to ward the devil off."

'I felt my flesh creep as he spoke. I'd heard the old folk say that devils roamed high up in the fells, but I'd never believed any of it.'

He paused – the faces round the fire were now fully attentive.

'But up there, just the two of us, and Jimmy so bloody jittery . . . I felt that anything could happen!'

'Surely, *you* couldn't have been scared Jackson? I can't imagine you being frightened of anything!" asked a disbelieving Tom.

'Circumstances alter things,' intoned Jackson solemnly. In front of a warm fire, sitting here among friends, we can

all laugh. . . But the fells can make you feel as though they are living giants, ready to swallow you up. . . And no one would find any trace of you, however hard they looked.'

'Was there a ghost? Whose grave was it?' asked Mary.

'Jimmy knew all about it. It was the grave of a packwoman who used to cross this Russet or whatever it's called Pass. She carried stuff to sell over in Langdale and suchlike places. If she died on that spot she must have had a great view as she gazed for the last time on the places she knew . . . poor soul.'

'You sound like a poet,' smiled Mary.

'Well, you've got to have some imagination when you think about things like that. The woman died after working like a slave all her life, scraping a bare living. . . And then these daft chaps from Langdale, Ambleside and Grasmere made the poor old thing out to be a ghost!'

'I would have felt a bit frightened too, if I'd been on that remote mountainside,' said Esther with a shiver. 'I've heard of ghosts like her appearing if their remains are not properly laid to rest . . . How long ago did she die, Dad?'

'Jimmy said they'd buried her properly up there about a hundred years ago, but local folk still feel uneasy when they pass by her grave. And some reckon that if you come down the pass a bit late, and it's getting dark, you can hear groans . . . just as if she's breathing her last. But I reckon she should have been well satisfied with her resting place. After all, she must have felt like dying a good many times when she was carrying her heavy pack over that pass . . . All this rubbish about ghosts has been invented by folk like Jimmy.'

'So how did you get on after you left the grave, Jackson?' asked Mary.

'Well, we came to Dungeon Ghyll . . . that's a name I've remembered for a good long time. The way Jimmy Marshall talked, I was sure we were just round the corner from his mother's house but, by God, we had another hour or two to go before we made it to her front door.'

'I'm sure she must have been pleased to see him,' said Edith.

'She was, because he hadn't been in touch since he'd left home.'

'Typical! You men don't think about anybody but yourselves.'

'None of us are much of a hand at writing letters, Esther . . . He was only a lad at the time and buying writing paper and pen and ink is a bit of a bother for the likes of us.'

'Fancy you being so far from home, Jackson,' smiled Tom. 'I didn't know you'd ever strayed so far from this area!'

'You should never take things for granted, Tom. Grasmere is a very interesting spot, with some good folk living in the district.'

'Especially in the pubs! I shouldn't think you met any in the churches!'

'You're right there, Mary. Church is where folk like to pretend they're something they're not, So I went to the pub in the middle of the main street where all the locals meet. I noticed that they get a lot of nosey visitors hanging about the village, looking for Wordsworth's cottage or some such place. I can never understand why intelligent folk spend money coming to see where somebody *used* to live! It's a damned sight livelier to have a crack with the living, especially in Grasmere . . . The folk I talked to in the pub reckoned his poetry was dreary and hard to understand, much like the chap himself.'

'That sounds a bit far-fetched. Wordsworth died long before anybody living there was born! How would they know anything about him?'

'Just like they do around here, Mary,' retorted Jackson. 'Haven't you heard the expression "within living memory"? We all know what our fathers and grandfathers said about folk who lived in Egremont long before our time, especially if it was a bit of scandal.'

'Pubs again! If it wasn't for the drinking man, most of our folklore would be lost without trace,' said Esther.

'It's a long time since I've heard you say anything as sensible as that,' observed Jackson. 'The locals had heard their parents and other folk who had worked for the gentry talking about what they were like.'

'A rich area is that,' remarked Bill who had been listening attentively to his father's story.

'Yes, but the goings on of the well-off didn't interest me very much.'

Jackson smiled as he remembered the crack in the pub so many years before. 'As I was saying,' he continued, 'the ordinary folk live much more interesting lives . . . Take dotterel-napping for instance.'

'Ditherer-napping!' laughed Bill in disbelief. 'What daft tale are you going to treat us to now, Dad?'

'I've never heard of a "ditherer", Jackson. What on

51

earth is it?' Tom, too was finding his friend's tales a bit hard to believe.

'I notice you're all prepared to listen to a tale that you reckon is a pack of lies. I can see by your faces! But, as sure as I'm sitting here, you can be sure that every word I'm going to utter is the truth.'

'Get on with the tale then,' urged Edith sceptically.

'A good and truthful story needs care in the telling, Edith. I might get the facts a bit muddled if you interrupt me. Now let me see . . . It was a chap called Tim who told me about the dotterels. Birds they are . . .'

'I've never heard of any such bird,' Bill remarked, lowering his paper.

'What do *you* know about rare birds, Bill?'

Bill knew better than to reply.

'You even got its name wrong. It's *dotterel*-napping, although I remember thinking at the time that "ditherer"

would be a better name for such a daft bird. Tim was telling me that this bird is rather rare and settles high up in the fells where it nests . . . As I was saying, the young chaps from Grasmere village go up the fellsides after work and enjoy a bit of dotterel-napping on a fine summer's evening.'

'What do they do, Dad?' asked Esther impatiently. 'What do you mean by "napping"?'

'Just what I say. You know how I give the dog a quick "nap" on its nose if it doesn't keep its mind on the job?'

She nodded.

'The young chaps used to walk up close to the birds, who didn't seem frightened of them . . . Then they napped them on the head! The birds didn't seem to have enough sense to fly away.'

'How can anybody amuse themselves by hitting a poor defenceless bird on the head?' said Edith disdainfully. 'They must be short of something to do if they go to all that trouble just to upset an innocent creature!'

'You don't understand these dalesmen, Edith. They put a lot of effort into their amusements,' explained Jackson patiently.

'I suppose it's no dafter than gurning through a horse's braffin, like they do in Egremont every back end,' laughed Tom.

'You *could* say that, Tom. But these dalesmen aren't a bit like us down here on the coast.

Tom nodded in agreement. 'That's right, Jackson. It's a well-known fact that the folk who live up the Borrowdale valley are a bit strange. . . They don't get called "Borrowdale cuckoos" for nothing.'

'Another unbelievable story coming up if you ask me,' laughed Mary.

'Oh no. Everybody can tell you about the Borrowdale cuckoos.'

'I've never heard of any such thing,' laughed Esther, 'but I'd like to hear about it.'

Tom settled to his subject, pleased to be able to tell a tale like Jackson's.

'The tale goes that a good few years back – further than anybody can remember now – the folk of Borrowdale noticed that when they heard the first cuckoo it meant that spring was on its way . . . But when the cuckoo left, the summer was over and they only had the bitter winter to look forward to. So they got the idea that if they built a barn for the cuckoo to live in, they could keep the good weather all year round!' Tom paused to see if his audience was paying attention.

'You don't expect us to believe such a daft tale?' said Bill.

'Let him finish,' urged Jackson.

'They got the barn almost finished. There was only the roof to put on . . . and then the cuckoo flew away.'

His listeners laughed.

'How could anybody be as stupid as that?' giggled Esther. 'It must be a really ancient story . . . No modern person would believe such a thing.'

'You can believe it or not, just as you please,' said Tom. But I can tell you that folk from Borrowdale are still called ''Borrowdale cuckoos'' to this very day. I expect the dotterel-nappers and the cuckoo catchers were communities that had grown up in isolated places and had intermarried, which, as all us farmers know, makes for weaknesses in the stock.'

He paused for a moment.

'That's why I married a lass from Whitehaven, A foreigner in the family can strengthen things up a lot,' observed Jackson.

'What did the ''nappers'' do with the birds they hit?'

'I should think they put them into a pie, Esther. That is, if they were good eating. If not, I reckon they went to a lot of bother for nothing. . . Us lowlanders don't waste our energy chasing uneatable quarry. We have a damned sight more sense!'

Tom nodded in agreement. 'Did you manage to find your way home then, Jackson?'

'I managed fine. The only upset was as I went past the old woman's grave without remembering to say a prayer. I almost stepped on a partridge which startled me so much I ran up the path lot faster than I had run down it a few days before!'

'Serves you right,' laughed Edith, 'for forgetting to say a prayer.'

'It's a funny thing,' continued Jackson, ignoring his wife's remark, 'but, like a Herdwick, I seemed to have no problem finding the right way back over the fells. I must have an inbuilt homing instinct.'

'Like the one I have now,' laughed Tom. 'It's time we were making our way back. I can see the snow lying thickly on your barn roof, Jackson, and if we wait much longer we'll have to dig our way out!'

'It's getting quite dark as well,' said Esther. 'At least you won't have to walk past any graves with ghosts hanging about.'

'Once I get past that tree where they say a bankrupt farmer once hanged himself I'll be much happier,' Mary said, with a shiver.

'It didn't bother you when you came earlier,' observed an amused Jackson.

'But that was in the daylight. They say ghosts only walk at night. . .'

'I don't think the only cuckoos live up in Borrowdale!' laughed Tom, following his nervous wife through the farmhouse door.

5

BETTY

'She looks very classy, Dad.'

Bill looked at the pony his father led from the stable. He eyed her up and down carefully. 'I like the colour – she'll look very smart pulling the milk cart. I bet she was expensive. I can see a definite streak of Arab in her.'

Jackson paused before replying. 'No, not really . . .'

'You bought her cheap, without a character? How on earth can Mam drive something we can't trust through the traffic and let our customers feed and pat her? Unless we put a public warning on her bridle!'

'The trouble with lads like you is that you daren't take a chance . . . If I'd always done what was safe I'd still be working down the pit, filling my lungs with dust. A bit of a pony like this one won't take a lot of handling. I've seen wickeder donkeys on the beach at Silloth, giving children rides.'

'What's her name?'

'The auctioneer said it was Betty.'

'Hello, Betty,' said Bill soothingly to the little pony. She turned her head immediately and looked invitingly in Bill's direction.

'Well, that's the first thing we've got right,' laughed Bill, stroking her nose gently. 'She looks too innocent to know any tricks, but a pony can outstrip any of the big horses when it comes to underhand, sneaky nastiness.'

He ran his hand gingerly over their new acquisition. 'My, but she's a lovely little thing, Dad. Look at them fine bones in her legs. I bet she's a neat mover – and that lovely strawberry coat will have all the customers coming to stroke her . . . You'd better fix a muzzle on her in case she likes to nip folks' hands when they feed her. Old Mrs Jenkinson never misses giving our horses an apple or a biscuit. The poor body would never get over it if this bonny little thing bit her. Customers don't expect a milk cart pony to have nasty habits.'

Jackson was disappointed at his son's reaction to his latest purchase, even though he knew Bill was right. He'd turned his back on common sense the minute he'd spotted this attractive little pony.

The mare swished her silky tail and reached out to nuzzle Bill's pocket for titbits, as though she'd followed the drift of the conversation. 'So, you're used to bribes,' smiled Bill, stroking her neck, but keeping a close watch on the two dangerous ends of the pretty animal.

'We'll hardly dare turn our backs on her, Dad, until we've worked out her personal "pedigree",' he said.

'I thought I'd wait until you got home before I harnessed her,' admitted Jackson. 'How about having a go now and seeing what she's like?'

'OK. I suppose a little thing like this can't do us much harm. Come on, Dad. Let's put the trap gear on her.'

Jackson was happy, now that Bill seemed to be falling under the spell of his new pony. They needed a new pony anyway, because Milly, the cob that took Edith on the milk round, was getting too slow and old. It was taking the pair of them half the day to deliver a few gallons of milk. But Edith was reluctant to part with Milly who knew every customer's door and had more experience of moving a cart and milk tins through the morning traffic than her town-bred driver did.

As though reading his thoughts, Bill asked, 'What does Mam think about Betty?'

'She's not happy but, as I've explained to her, one of these fine days Milly is likely to drop down dead as they pull up Kell Head Hill, and then what will she do? This little mare will carry her to Egremont and back in half the time it takes her now.'

Bill nodded his head doubtfully. 'I'm glad it's you who has to persuade her and not me. She's always relied on being able to let Milly walk along without having to keep hold of the reins while she delivers from the back of the trap. You'll have to go with her for a week or two until Betty learns the ropes . . . and good luck to you!'

The first yoking of an unknown horse always presents problems - backs have to be turned cautiously, kicks and bites have to be anticipated. There was an air of tension in the farmyard as the two men placed the trap gear on to the pony.

Betty moved obligingly to accommodate their every move, obviously familiar with the ceremony.

At last she stood ready to be backed between the shafts of the milk trap. Her large liquid eyes seemed to be questioning their unease.

'Now for the tricky bit,' said Jackson. But the trap was secured without any fuss.

'Take her for a walk around the yard, lad, and see if she has any objection to pulling the cart.'

Betty obliged by pulling the trap, first empty, then loaded with rattling tins.

'Lovely! Now let's climb aboard and try a trot down the road and see how well-behaved she is.'

Indeed, the new pony passed the test with flying colours, returning home with milk tins and passengers all safe, and full of praise for the little mare's performance.

Jackson accompanied the timid Edith for a couple of weeks, but very soon Betty had learnt where to stop. She knew every customer, especially Mrs Jenkinson who swore that she and Betty had an understanding, the pony having soon spotted the pocket where the old lady kept her apples and sweets. They pony also had a way of gently whinnying at children on their way to school as well as to other people she had learnt to recognise.

'That pony'll get us more customers than any amount of

advertising,' laughed Jackson one evening as they were having their supper.

'There must be some mystery about her though,' observed Edith. 'To be sold at such a low price, I don't trust her . . . There must be something wrong somewhere.'

'It's always the same with you women,' snarled Jackson. 'You have no faith in my eye for horses. The little lady has been badly handled, that's all . . . She's found a good home and she's grateful. Not like some of you women, who find fault with everything a chap tries to do for you.'

Edith felt a bit chastened. 'I suppose you're right. Maybe I haven't given you enough credit. Perhaps her previous owner was very young and didn't treat her kindly.'

'He must have known something about breaking in horses,' said Bill, as he tackled his eggs and bacon. 'She seems to know the ropes well enough . . . and she's a treat to drive.'

'Yes, lad, and you'd better watch out. I heard you were racing her down Egremont Main Street last Thursday afternoon.'

'Which nosey parker bothered to tell you that I gathered a bit of speed. It was a job to slow her down . . . The trap was empty and she knew she was on the way home.'

'Never mind who it was . . . The same good friend told me that that keen young policeman they've sent to Egremont has been cautioning one or two drivers of the smarter-looking traps for exceeding the speed limit and driving to the danger of the public.'

Edith looked alarmed. 'Be careful, son,' she warned, 'I wouldn't like to read your name in the *Whitehaven News* for dangerous driving. What on earth would the neighbours think? And our May! She'd never get over the disgrace!'

'That would make it worthwhile,' laughed Jackson gleefully. 'She might even decide to go and live down south again, to get away from the criminal element in her family!'

* * *

The following Sunday Edith set off on the milk round as usual. It was a fine morning, and Betty's hooves sounded sharp and willing on the surface of the road. Nothing had ever persuaded Milly to increase her speed – she had known that her mistress lacked the strengh of will to urge her to a better performance. But this little pony only needed the reins to be shaken ever so slightly to produce a surge of speed. Edith glanced along the shining well-brushed spine, the leather straps shaking lightly over the smooth coat and wondered, as she often did, at the endurance and strength of such a small animal. How could she trot without stopping for mile after mile, pulling a loaded trap?

She had to admit that this new milk pony was a pleasure to handle and, best of all, she returned home much earlier than she used to with Milly. Poor Milly. Edith felt guilty at her pleasure with her new pony. After all, the older pony had given years of faithful service.

However Milly was going as a first pony to a little girl who lived up Wilton way, so she would have an easier life among people who would love and care for her.

Edith enjoyed the Sunday delivery. Most people were on their way to church at this time of day. She liked to see the children in their Sunday best waving as the pony trotted by. There was always a feeling of holiday on a bright sunny Sunday morning.

Soon Edith only had the vicarage left to visit. She was glad it was her last port of call, because it was a good pull up the hill. And now that the cart was almost empty, the load was kinder to the pony.

As usual on a Sunday, the vicarage was deserted. No one came out with a jug to be filled, the whole family having gone to church early. Edith left the cart and walked over to the doorstep to collect the jug to fill with milk and the smaller jug to fill with cream for their Sunday tea.

She was just completing her task when she heard a sharp rattle and then the clatter of shafts striking the gravelled driveway, followed by the drumming of galloping hooves as Betty streaked out through the open vicarage gates and headed down the hill!

Edith glanced at the trap, its shafts still quivering from the shock of being dropped so quickly. The leather gear was scattered in a short line in the wake of the departing pony. Nothing remained on Betty's back – even her bridle lay where it had been shaken off.

Edith picked up the broken bridle and dashed after the mare. What if she reaches the main street and frightens the women and children? she thought, hurrying as fast as she could after the disappearing animal.

'Here you are, Missus,' called a voice from the lane that ran from the end of the main road to a farm.

'Thank God you spotted her,' gasped Edith. 'Could you help me harness her again? I'm not very good if the pony is awkward.'

'Certainly, Mrs Strong,' said the man, who recognised the milk woman.

'I don't know what got into her. She has been such a well-behaved pony so far. I don't know what Jackson will say when I get home. . .'

'Just so long as you are unhurt, he won't mind. . .'

'Don't you believe it, Mr Kitchen. He doesn't think I'm any good with stock . . . and he's right. They have to be very well-mannered before I can manage them. Besides, a horse is a more valuable asset than a wife. You should know that, being local.'

'Don't talk such rubbish! Come on and I'll have a go at repairing this bridle and fixing the cart so that you can drive home safely,' said Derek Kitchen to the worried Edith.

Very soon he had the pony securely strapped to the milk cart and drove Edith to the edge of the town. He stood and watched her drive the now happy mare in the direction of home.

* * *

'It appears that your new pony has made you famous throughout the district, Jackson,' commented Abe Mossop when the regulars at the Grey Mare had all settled themselves to their pints.

'Why's that?' asked Jackson innocently.

'You seem to have bought a shaker,' Abe announced to the listening drinkers. 'I heard that the only things she wore when she bolted from the vicarage front door were her shoes. And if she'd found time she would have had them off as well . . .'

'I reckon she should have been called Houdini,' chuckled Alan Steel. 'And, as if Sunday's performance at the vicarage wasn't enough, I heard that your Bill was stopped right in front of the Co-op bakery department and warned about speeding . . .'

'The way things are going, that pony'll cost you more than a better one would have done at that sale,' laughed Joe Watson.

'What do you shopkeepers know about buying and selling horses? Us farmers have to take chances . . . like we do with owt else. We have to stand the loss of poor crops, while you chaps just glance at our stuff and say, "them taties won't sell". You simply turn your back on what we've spent months working on, and leave us to stand the loss . . . Your job's just window-dressing if you ask me!'

'Why don't you admit that you were just taken in by a smart-looking animal?' jibed Alan.

'She's smart all right, Alan . . . She's learning fast this week.'

'What on earth are you doing to the poor little thing? I hope you aren't being cruel to her to teach her a lesson.'

'How could you think such a thing, Jean? The best thing

to do with a shaker is to keep her moving. It's only when she stands still that she can shake all the gear off. Her feet have hardly touched the ground for the last week!'

'So we hear,' laughed Alan gleefully. 'The queue outside the Co-op bakery can all testify to that!'

'It's a pity they didn't all stay at home and do a bit of baking,' snapped Jackson. 'Even our Edith buys the odd cake from the bakery van that's started to come round. Since we've had electricity put in, our womenfolk have become lazy . . . They seem to have nowt better to do then gawp at a young policeman making a fool of himself in the middle of the main street.'

'That's not the way I heard it.'

'No, I bet it wasn't . . . Our Bill had *finished* his morning's work when he was stopped. I mean that young policeman was simply looking around for something to occupy his mind, making a good *start* to his day, trying to impress a few idle, gossiping women. Now if he'd gone looking for some of them lads that hang around the pubs of a night, drinking too much of their fathers' money, that would have pleased the whole town. But no, speeding traffic is an easy catch. The lads would have told him to bugger off anyway!'

'Come on now, Jackson. Fair's fair. If your lad was exceeding the speed limit then the policeman was only doing his duty. The police have to consider the safety of those citizens who have difficulty crossing the street. You know yourself how wide it is.'

'Yes, I know how wide the street is . . . and I also know that there's one law for the rich and influential, and another for us ordinary folk.'

'What do you mean?' asked Jean. 'As far as I know, the law of the land applies equally – to us all.'

'That's where you're wrong, lass. Just you imagine Lord Lonsdale driving through in one of his Rolls-Royces . . . Can you see an eager young policeman daring to put his hand up, especially in front of a crowd of women shoppers? No, the minute the policeman spots a polished crest, he turns the other way to move the traffic out of his lordship's path.'

Jean laughed. 'Surely you wouldn't expect someone like him to be treated like a common criminal? After all, he owns most of the county!'

'There you are,' nodded an aggrieved Jackson. 'One law for his lordship, and another for a chap who can only afford to buy second-best horses.'

'I reckon you've been landed with third or fourth-best,' tittered a delighted Alan Steel.

Jackson moved his chair over to the domino table with a dismissive air, the episode of the pony already ancient history.

'Just tell me then, Jackson, if you were a lord and had to choose a coat of arms, what would it be?'

'That's an easy one Alan. What else could it be, but a stallion and a bull . . . rampant, of course!'

6

A REGIMENT OF DUCKS

The door of the Grey Mare slammed shut behind the young soldier.

'You're late, Brian,' remarked his two uniformed friends, already ensconced close to the fire with their glasses of beer.

'He'll have been chasing some girl or other,' laughed Dave, taking another swig of his beer.

'Don't mention women to me, Dave. I learnt my lesson earlier on tonight,' said Brian ruefully.

'Oh, did you? Something desperate must have happened if you've been persuaded to give up the chase. Tell us about it, Brian,' he urged. 'It's sure to be a tale worth hearing.'

Jackson Strong, who was playing dominoes by the window, laid down his hand and looked in the direction of the three young soldiers. 'The British Army has never been the same since women were called up,' he pronounced. 'The battles in the Middle Ages were the most sensible – it was all over in an afternoon, and those who were still alive could go back home and get on with their lives in peace. I can't understand how this government can waste good money paying your wages just to allow you to run after women soldiers.'

'At the princely sum of a shilling a day, I don't think it'll break the national bank!' laughed the young soldier.

'That's right,' nodded Tom, ignoring the last remark. 'I've surprised a few couples in that far field of ours near the camp. I can't understand how they can spend time mucking about in the middle of the afternoon!'

'Come on then, Brian. Tell us what you've been up to.'

Brian settled himself alongside his friends, with a pint

close to his right hand. 'It was one of them Italian POWs that caused all the trouble . . . ' he began.

'I can't believe any of them Italians could possibly do anything underhand, Brian,' Tom interrupted. 'We've always found them polite, pleasant and helpful when they come to work on our farm. In fact I don't consider the Italians to be fighters at all – at least not in the same way the Germans are. No, it would take a lot to persuade me that one of them had harmed you.'

'It isn't what they do at all, Tom,' answered the young soldier. It's the fact that all the women find them attractive, especially the women officers . . . Good Englishmen don't have a cat in hell's chance when them "I'ties" are around the place!'

It's a question of politeness and good manners,' interrupted Jean from behind the bar. 'They aren't as rough and ignorant as many of the lads around here. You can't blame nice girls for taking a shine to them – they know how to speak to a woman.'

'A load of rubbish!' snarled Jackson, looking up from his dominoes. 'Them chaps have to learn their English from a book, and there were no dirty words in the books we read at school. The folk who write books aren't like us. They live in spots like London and talk the King's English so that everybody will be able to understand one another if they have to travel, or fight in the war. You must remember that we've all got to be able to understand the officers in charge, or there might be confusion on the battlefield . . .'

'I can't follow the point you're making, Jackson . . .' said Jean, looking puzzled.

'He means that women are easily taken in by a few fancy words that we've never got round to using even if we understood them,' explained Tom.

Jackson nodded. 'If I made my meaning clear to you, Tom, then Jean should have known what I was saying. Women tend to judge a parcel by its packaging . . . They get taken in every time by a glib tongue and a foreign accent.'

'That's right, Jackson. They never stop to think how many wives those POWs might have left at home in Italy!'

'What a silly thing to say, Tom,' laughed Jean. 'Italians are very religious. Most of them are Catholic and wouldn't dream of having more than one wife.'

'It's you that's silly, Jean,' snapped Jackson impatiently. 'You women are slow to learn that a wife at home nice and safe is very religious; but mucking about with someone else's in a foreign land, especially in wartime, is perfectly all right.'

'Spoils of war, they call it,' added Dave.

'Trust you lot to read something bad into it all. You just can't take any opposition,' retorted Jean.

'Anyway, get on with your story, Brian. Tell us about the handsome Italian POW.'

Brian smiled a bit grimly and began his tale for the second time.

'As I was telling you, I set off from the camp, taking a short cut through a hole in the back fence and then across the farmer's field which leads on to the main road close to your farm, Jackson. It saves a lot of time.'

'You're like all the rest of them,' lamented Tom, reaching for his pint. 'God help us if Gerry ever reaches these shores. I reckon we'll have to rely on ourselves . . . You soldiers will all be too busy escaping to meet some woman.'

'Let him carry on, Tom,' interrupted Dave, who wanted to hear what had happened next.

'Well, I was stumbling about in the dark, trying to find the path, when I slipped and started to slide slowly down into a ditch.'

'Serves you right,' growled Jackson, 'Clambering about in a chap's fields . . . God knows what rubbish I'll find when I come to clean them dyke-backs out!'

'You're welcome to what I slid on to in that ditch, Jackson.'

Jackson was now alarmed at the prospect of something dangerous in one of his ditches. 'Tell us about it, lad. I thought us farmers were fighting Hitler and *his* chaps . . . I didn't expect to have to fight the British Army as well!'

'No, nothing like that, Jackson. Nothing so straightforward. As I was sliding down, I realised that there was someone lying at the bottom . . . Or rather, there were two people!'

'Now it's getting more interesting,' laughed Dave.

'All I could see,' continued Brian, 'was a dirty big yellow circle, so I knew it was one of Mussolini's romeos on top!'

Brian now had the attention of the entire bar. Pints were lowered to assist the listening process.

'Didn't you shift him out of there pretty quickly then?' asked Tom.

'After all, he's only a prisoner of war. You could have ordered him to clear off.'

'I didn't have time to speak . . . That bloody toffee-nosed ATS officer with the big bosoms, the one that has a certain way of looking at any chap she fancies, was suddenly fixing me with a stare that could have killed at thirty paces. "Clear the hell out of this, *soldier*," she snapped. "And that's an order." '

The audience rocked with laughter.

'Didn't you find time to tell her she was improperly dressed, Brian?'

'No, Dave, I didn't. I reckon she would have put me on a charge as soon as look at me, even though she was lying down in a field with her dignity more than a little compromised.'

'Quite right to beat a retreat,' chuckled Jackson. 'A good man knows when he's been beaten by a better woman!'

Tom nodded, 'It's a fact, Jackson. I've heard you say many a time that the female of any species is the stronger.'

'It's just a pity the fighting woman can't seem to

remember who the enemy is!' moaned the aggrieved Brian.

'Of course she can,' laughed Jackson. 'The enemy is the chap she doesn't fancy at that moment, who might get in the way of her getting the one she's really after. It's the same in peacetime. Their aims are different from ours. They are led by their emotions, not by anyone in fancy brass buttons!'

'Heaven help all of us,' snapped Jean from behind the bar, 'if we are to be saved by any of you lot!'

The evening wore on and the laughter slowly died down in the snug pub. Soon Jackson felt the need to liven things up a bit. 'For goodness sake put some more coal on that fire, Jean. It's as cold back here as sitting on a slow horse in a blizzard.'

'When did you ever sit on a horse in a blizzard, Jackson?' challenged one of the regulars. The farmer paused, holding the dominoes he was about to lay on the table.

'I've survived a few nasty snowstorms in my time, especially when I worked up in Wasdale. And I was never so daft as to ride a bloody horse . . . I've always reckoned that it's better to get back home alive and buggered than let the horse find its own way back with you dead – frozen to its so-called comfortable saddle.'

'I can't understand why you should freeze to death on the saddle in the first place, Jackson,' observed Alan Steel as he slowly placed his next domino on the table.

'Too cold. It stands to reason, Alan. It's as good as sitting out on the fellside in an armchair, and even *you* wouldn't think of doing owt as daft as that, now would you?'

'I suppose not,' he agreed warily, a little afraid that the old man was leading him into some sort of trap.

'No. A struggle with the wind and the cold will keep you alive a lot longer than sitting up on top with your blood running colder and colder.'

Glancing up towards the bar he noticed that Jean the

barmaid was still listening attentively and hadn't moved a muscle since he'd asked for the coal.

'Well, lass, are you going to stand there and watch me freeze to death in my own local, for want of a shovel of coal?'

'It would be more gentlemanly of you to get up and throw some coal on the fire yourself. You can't expect all women to wait on you hand and foot like your Edith does,' laughed Joe Watson.

'I've never lifted a shovelful of the bloody stuff since I left the pit, Joe. You don't think I'd shovel it for nowt? Besides, I'm not a shopkeeper like you – I don't have to please all the women in the district. It does the womenfolk good to see what dirty jobs some of us men have to do to keep them in comfort in their nice warm houses.'

'Thank your lucky stars, Jackson, that your Edith doesn't come in here for a drink. She'd have something to say about remarks like that!'

'I've got my wife well trained, don't you worry. I was wise enough to marry a woman with a religious turn of mind . . . You can't go wrong with a wife who believes every word you say, and thinks we're so busy playing cards and drinking in the pub that we don't have time to think of chasing other women . . . Our Edith always boasts that she knows exactly where I am, and she's never wrong.'

'So you're never tempted to chase someone else's wife then?' asked Joe, still stung by Jackson's derogatory remarks about shopkeepers.

'No, never. I have enough trouble managing the one I've got. Life is complicated enough as it is. Farmers have to work at home and a good wife is one who's willing to work, doesn't ask too many daft questions and minds her own business . . . Flighty women aren't like that. You have to spend all day telling them how good they look and all night making sure you don't leave them on their own in case they leave you for some other chap who isn't satisfied with what he's got . . . Oh, no, I like to be able to spend the night in the pub, knowing that my wife is busy finishing a hookey mat or a quilt. Don't worry, Joe, I've got my life sorted out very comfortably . . . Ah, that's better Jean. That fire'll light up the dark corners of the pub quite nicely and then I might be able to see what domino Alan's just sneaked on to the table.'

'Our John's late tonight,' observed Alan, attempting to divert Jackson's attention from the game.

'It's your turn to lay, Alan. Don't worry yourself about your John. He won't have finished milking them Friesians of his yet. He's managed to have most of them calving at the same time like he usually does . . . That expensive bull he bought a couple of years ago nearly has a nervous breakdown when they all want bulling at the same time. And for nearly six months of the year he thinks he's a bullock! John's lucky that Friesian bulls are so good-natured. If he'd bought a Shorthorn bull like mine, he wouldn't have dared go near it if it hadn't had any work for a few weeks.'

'Come on, Jackson, let's finish the game. You're wasting good drinking time cracking on about John's cows, and you don't know what on earth you're talking about. Our John spends a lot of time and money improving his pedigree herd. The milk cheque he gets at the end of the month is probably one of the best in the district.'

'I'm sure it is, Alan. It's just that it'll change faster than the weather forecast.'

The door of the pub opened and a couple of regulars, Sid and Sam Thompson, made their way first to the bar, then to their usual seats near the domino table.

'By God it's cold tonight,' announced Sid, trying to warm both hands at the welcome flames as well as balance his pint of bitter.

'You're bloody lucky to be able to get a decent warm at that fire, Sid,' chuckled Jackson. 'If it hadn't been for me stirring Jean into some sort of action ten minutes ago you would have risked a dose of pneumonia. These easy-living publicans don't know how chaps like you sweat your guts out below ground hacking iron ore and coal to make somebody else's life a bit easier. They never think how near the fires of hell you work; how, when you come up on top, the cold weather cuts through you like a knife through butter. You should be thankful that somebody like me has been thinking about you and making sure there's a warm welcome waiting for you.'

'Stop mollycoddling them, Jackson,' protested Alan Steel. 'Pitmen are as tough as we are. Don't make out that a couple of invalids have managed to walk all the way from Egremont. They've a better colour than I have, and I spend my days out of doors.'

'Colour! Colour!' retorted the old farmer. 'Since when has colour in the iron ore mines ever been a good guide to health? If you worked all your life in red muck you might have a nice pink glow on your face! The trouble is that it won't wash off. It's worse on the inside an' all . . . Just ask any of these healthy-looking chaps to spit for you and you'll see that their insides are redder than their outsides! Why do you think I packed in working down the mines? Swallowing dust for nigh on twenty years was enough for me. I fancied the life of a gentleman.'

'Let's hope you will be one . . . in time, Jackson!' Alan replied tartly.

'I've never heard such wise words uttered in a pub before in my life,' said Sam Thompson as he lit his pipe. 'Usually outsiders think we have a soft, well-paid job – only working half the day, then spending most of our time racing pigeons or hound dogs.'

'Shut your bloody mouth will you, Sam' hissed Jackson. 'Don't you think I've said enough to get them going without you firing the bullets for them? Come to think of it, I didn't hear myself say that the mining companies employed the pick of the brains in the district! Some folk don't know when they're getting a leg up.'

As Jackson finished his speech the door of the Grey Mare opened, the wind whipping in along with John Steel and Abe Mossop.

'My God, what a wild night! Come on, Abe, let's get a warm up and a pint to slake our dry throats,' said the younger man.

'Nice to see you both,' said Jean pulling pints for the two farmers.

'We nearly had a bit of an accident on the way here!' laughed John as he and his friend settled themselves down in the warmth of the now blazing fire.

'An accident? How on earth could you have an accident? All the dangerous drivers in the district are sitting here in the pub,' Jackson observed.

'Well, I drive better drunk than sober,' said John. 'At least, that's what folk tell me.'

'That's right,' nodded Abe. 'I reckon John can leave this pub and make it through that narrow farmyard gate of his without touching either gatepost, but he's made plenty of scrape marks on them during the day!'

'I seem to remember that there were no marks on John's gateways before he bought himself a motorcar. For years, when he and his father before him had only horses to work with, there were no marks at all on them stones.'

'Are you trying to tell us, Jackson, that after all these years of complaining that the Steels were only moderate horsemen, now you're admitting they weren't so bad after all?'

'I'm saying no such thing, Abe. What I *am* saying is that the Steels always bought a decent horse, an intelligent horse, one that could negotiate the gateways, whether or not the chap on top had any notion of what he was doing. A clever horse is a necessity for farmers like them.'

'I seem to remember many a time when one or other of your horses had to carry you home, drunk as a lord, lying in the back after some good landlord had pushed you into the cart and slapped the horse on its backside. You were thankful yourself to have a clever horse then!'

'When a chap's drunk, allowances have to be made – we all understand that – but to be stone-cold sober and crack a stone stoop with a motorcar wheel must mean that the driver had to rely on the horses before he bought the car. After all, a car is easier to drive through a narrow gateway than a horse is. It doesn't get fatter or make a beeline for the stable door if it's hungry.'

'What accident did you just avoid then, John?' asked his brother.

'Well, Abe and me were driving along slowly when we came to Jackson's farm, and we had to stop . . . in a bit of a hurry like.'

'My farm? I can't think of any stock that we didn't fasten up before I left home. What made you stop, John?'

'Well, we came round the corner into the village, and there they were, wandering down the middle of the road as though it was first thing in the morning.'

'You mean Jackson's ducks?' Tom asked.

'Yes, cackling and waddling along in a straight line . . . I reckon they were hungry and were on their way down to the beck to have a paddle about.'

'My ducks hungry?' exclaimed Jackson, sounding injured. 'My ducks are quite able to look after themselves. What do you think they have wings for? Our Muscovies can fly anywhere in the district to find food.'

'Well, they didn't seem keen on flying tonight. We had to slow down for them.'

'They knew they were in no danger. I'm not worried about them, John . . . I have them trained.'

'How do you mean "trained", Jackson? I've never heard of anyone training ducks! Don't tell us that duck-training is part of your farming programme?'

'Of course it is . . . Surely you train your poultry! If you have animals that need to walk on the roads as part of their

feeding routine then it's necessary to train them in safety on the public highway.'

'You mean a duck highway code?' asked an amused Sid. 'I've never managed to train our hound dogs to walk on their own – we have to pay a "walker" . . . Let us into your secret, Jackson, and we'll make a fortune training dogs to take themselves for walks.'

'It's ducks we're discussing at the moment. Dogs are a different sort of animal. Besides, taking ducks out on leads in the same way as dogs would be a bit daft, not to say a waste of time for a busy farmer. No, ducks can be trained easily enough. But how can a chap talk with a dry throat?'

A pint was duly ordered by Sid and Sam who were interested in learning how to exercise their hounds with the least possible expense.

'Come on then, Jackson. Let's hear how you trained your ducks.'

'First of all, it takes quite a bit of observation. As with any sort of training, you've got to know something about the natural habits of the animal. The duck, as you may have noticed, is like a woman.'

'Here we go! Something stupid about women. I might have guessed,' called Jean from behind the bar. 'In any case, I understand that it's Edith who looks after the poultry on your farm, just like most farmers' wives do.'

'Stop changing the subject, Jean. We're waiting to hear the rest of this unlikely tale,' said John impatiently.

'Those of you who keep ducks,' continued Jackson, 'will know that you only need to train one of them. When that's done, others will copy and follow on, in line . . . just like women, as I said. If one woman wears the latest fashion in coats, for instance, then every woman in the neighbourhood has to turn out in the same thing – or else she gets talked about . . . At least that's what my daughters tell me when they want some money for a new coat or dress. And ducks are exactly the same – copycats!'

'Which duck do you choose to train then, Jackson?' asked a serious-faced Sid.

'You town-bred lads won't know that ducks and cows always have a leader, one that always likes to be at the front and won't allow any of the others to pass her.'

'I notice you said "her",' Jean pointed out. 'You wouldn't have such a keen audience if you talked about what bullies most men are.'

'You keep quiet, my lass, or we'll see about getting a man behind that bar, someone who will take an intelligent interest in the crack in here.'

'Just carry on, then,' scoffed Jean, 'talking the rubbish we usually hear on a Saturday night.'

'She's got a point, Jackson,' suggested Sid. '*Is* it always a female who leads the pack?'

'Ninety-nine times out of a hundred, Sid. Just like humans, we think we get our own way but of course we never do . . . Ducks naturally haven't got the sophistication of our wives. No, they just take the lead and the poor chaps have no option but to follow on behind . . . exactly like us well-trained husbands.'

The laughter drifted warmly around the old pub, and Jackson glanced at the faces of his audience, mostly hard-working farmers and miners – always ready to listen to his observations, whether they were true or false.

'Our leading duck'll be a good age now – at least ten years old she'll be and never had a handful of corn thrown in her direction. If we were daft enough to feed her that would be the end of a decent bite of duck at Christmas-time for a few folk in Egremont. A duck that's fed in the yard by the farmer's wife isn't worth the time and effort spent lighting a fire to cook it. No, a muscovy that's wandered abut to find its food in the natural way makes a real tasty dinner.'

'What about this training then, Jackson? How's it done?'

'It's a simple enough matter, Sid. A young inexperienced farmer might be tempted to choose a young bird to train, but that would be wrong . . . The oldest female is the one that knows how things work on the farm.'

'And the one that's learnt to get out of your way before you run over it with the horse and cart, eh, Jackson?'

'I never knew you had that much idea about things, John. Of course you're right . . . A duck has to be shown the dangers in the farmyard first, then it'll listen for cars and traffic on the road and automatically get out of the way in good time. I don't really train my ducks – they just learn to look out for themselves and those that survive warn the others. And as ducks walk in single file behind the leader, it's easier for them all to do the right thing. Now if your hound dogs walked in single file you wouldn't have such problems with them. Most bloody trail hounds need a nose full of aniseed before they know if they're going backwards or forwards. By God, I've seen a woman walking hounds with as many as ten leads all mixed up in her hands. She daren't let them off or she'd never set eyes on them for a fortnight!'

'There's some truth in that, Jackson,' laughed Sid. 'Hound dogs have no sense of direction. But I don't think we have much chance of training them like your ducks.'

* * *

On Saturday night the following week John and Abe were once again making their way to the Grey Mare.

The car slowed down as it reached the corner near Jackson's farm.

'Look, there's those bloody ducks of Jackson's waddling down the middle of the road as if they own the entire district,' exclaimed Abe.

'Just like their owner,' replied John. 'I know . . . Let's put Jackson's training to the test!'

'What do you mean? You wouldn't deliberately run over his ducks to prove he was making it all up?'

John didn't reply. He just pressed his foot on the accelerator.

* * *

Sunday was always a day when something special found its way to Edith's table.

'Well, Mother, I did enjoy that bit of duck. It's a change to have something different, even if it's not quite Christmastime yet.'

'We wouldn't have had it if you'd made sure the ducks were fastened in before you finished milking. They wander up and down the roads like lost tramps . . . I'm not surprised one got knocked down. You can't expect drivers to see a row of stupid ducks in the half-light wandering home from a long afternoon down the beck. You've let them get into lazy habits. I wonder who it was'

She looked anxiously at her husband. 'Just so long as the person wasn't upset about it.'

'He wouldn't have been half as upset as this young duck was when a stupid bloody driver couldn't recognise a row of ducks arse-on.'

Edith cleared away the dishes, shaking her head at Jackson's carelessness. 'Isn't it about time you moved out of that chair if you're going to the pub tonight? You seem to be settling yourself very comfortably by the fire . . . and is that a copy of the *Farmers' Weekly* I see in your hand?'

'Can't a chap spend a night at home by his own fire without being cross-examined as to what his motives might be?' remarked Jackson tetchily.

'No, it's just a bit surprising. You only miss a Sunday night at the Grey Mare if you're ill. I know how much you enjoy a crack with the folk from Egremont.'

'Well, they can enjoy their fun in the pub without me

this Sunday night. You'd think I made a habit of entertaining the entire countryside!'

7

SEEDS AND SHOES

Fine, not too crisp mornings, are precious to farmers. Rain makes the soil too heavy to be ploughed. Frost makes it equally difficult to cut through, even with the keenest of ploughs and work horses. Just right is one of those days when the already ploughed earth is dry enough to be harrowed easily, and the recently turned sods rattle through the fast-moving teeth of the farmer's harrow. Drier land means easier pulling for the horses, less urging from the driver, and a finer soil bed for the seeds.

This was just such a true Spring morning.

'Come on, Jane,' called Jackson to his elder daughter. 'Hurry up and finish your breakfast. It's time you were off. Yon ten acre needs to be harrowed today. Tomorrow might be wet.'

'OK Dad, but I had to help you with the milking. I can't leave an old man like you to do it alone – even with that new milking machine!'

'Don't be so cheeky, my lass. I don't need any help – and not so much of the "old". I can work as long as you young 'uns. At your age I would have had half that field done by this time of the morning.'

'It's only half-past nine.'

'Half-past nine? It's very nearly coffee time,' snarled Jackson.

'Never you mind, Jane,' soothed her mother. 'Get the horses and start work. I'll walk to the field with a nice drink and some cake for you at about eleven.'

'Then she'll have to come home for dinner at twelve,' snorted Jackson. 'The horses won't know whether they're at work or on holiday.'

Jane ignored her father's remarks and went to catch

Peggy and Dolly. Both these mares were Clydesdales – used for work and breeding – and each one produced a foal most years. Good mares were kept to breed, while their foals were raised, broken in to farm work, then sold.

Horses were another valuable cash crop. Even when 'in foal', mares had to earn their keep, so they were worked as long as possible – often until their bellies were too big to fit between the shafts of the carts.

An eleven-month gestation period meant that a breeding mare was 'in foal' within a month of the birth of her last foal. Harrowing, grubbing and ploughing was all chain work, so none of the restrictions of pregnancy applied there.

Once foaled, the mares still had little respite; it was the practice to return them to their work as soon as possible. The foal was left in a loose box, to be fed when its mother returned home at dinnertime. Then it rejoined her at the end of the working day.

Foaling could be a hazardous . . . and for a small farmer, the death of one of his two work horses could mean the end of his livelihood – that is, if he didn't have a spare horse to make up his basic draught of two. If this happened, the farmer had to borrow a horse from a kind neighbour, or buy a new one.

One of the finest sights during April and May was the team of huge Clydesdale entires (stallions) which walked long distances from their base at Lockerbie to serve the mares over a very wide area of southern Scotland and northern England. Often making a round trip of 100 miles or so, they were fed and accommodated at night in farms *en route*.

The arrival of the entire was another of the seasonal 'events' marking the progress of the farming year. A huge, beautiful beast, his regal, arched neck proclaimed his power as he jostled his bit on his handler's hand. A plaited and beribboned mane and tail often added the finishing touches. His saddle and bridle were polished with so much care, catching the Spring sunlight – the entire was his own walking advert!

Each year the newest stallion would be looked over and admired, its handler having groomed its coat until it gleamed, the white feathery hair on its lower legs accentuating its force and speed.

* * *

Jane hooked the chains to the tugs which were to pull the harrows across the newly ploughed field. Soil is not fine enough after ploughing – it needs to be harrowed at least once before it is sown with a cereal crop or 'stitched' up into furrows for potato and vegetable crops.

Horses are intelligent creatures, and, like most of us, they don't really like hard work. The farmer controlled them by means of thin ropes tied to their bits, then passed

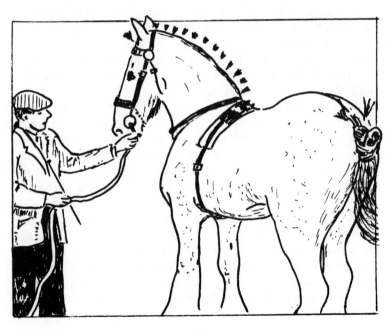

through rings on the side of the narrow strap saddles. In Cumberland these ropes were called 'cords'. Ploughing cords and a coupling cord, which linked the two horses together, formed the basic 'steerage'.

The horses knew by the way the cords were handled just how capable the human at the other end was. A passing visitor who asked to 'have a go' would find that the horses refused to take a single step. Threats, rope-shaking and desperate pleas would all be ignored by the disdainful beasts, much to the amusement of the farmer.

The minute Jackson Strong picked up their cords, they were off, pulling strongly, striding together in a lively rhythm. But they kept a hopeful eye and ear on the road, where, with luck, they might spot one of their master's friends.

The command to stop was totally unnecessary. Having spotted the master's friend, all eight feet would come to a halt in the same split second, their noses instantly buried in the tasty, hitherto forbidden grass! They had been listening hopefully ever since the start of the day's work for the sound of a footstep, or the equally welcome brisk hoofbeats of neighbouring 'friends'.

Jane, however, was completely different from Jackson. They knew she loved them and they knew she was weaker than her father, so they could trail their feet to gain sympathy. They could slow down – from sheer exhaustion of course. Juicy mouthfuls were snatched from the hedgerows at every turn.

They knew exactly when her clogs had filled up with sharp stones and gritty soil. The slightest of limps produced by this discomfort resulted in an immediate, *sympathetic* halt to the work. Crafty noses tended to veer, ever so slightly, in a gatewards direction as they faced home.

The whole scene was enlivened by the wheeling sea-gulls, appearing from nowhere and swooping only inches behind her weary feet to seize the shiny, freshly disinterred worms, their calls screeching a challenge to the border collie as he raced ahead of the horses, then returned to check on his mistress. Amused rabbits, too, watched the proceedings from the safety of their burrows, only disappearing at the last minute, their white fluffy tails nodding defiance at the frustrated dog.

'Just look at that bloody field,' Jackson Strong complained to his friend Tom Graham as the two farmers leant on the gate.

The horses and their driver were moving round the edge of the field at a very brisk pace. Peggy and Dolly knew that this process finished the work off neatly . . . and heralded their release.

'Not a straight line in sight! I hope it rains tonight before the neighbours see what a bloody mess she's made of it.'

The horses reached the gate, hauling an exhausted Jane in their wake.

'That's a good job done, Jane.'

'Thanks, Mr Graham. Oh my poor feet, they don't half ache!'

Jackson ran his hands down Peggy's leg, then lifted her nearside leg. 'Look at this,' He held the offending hoof up for his daughter to inspect. 'This shoe is very slack. I think we'll have to get it fixed before she does any more work.'

Peggy pulled eagerly to release her foot . . . home beckoned! The two horses crowded against the gate as Jackson tried to push it open. All trace of tiredness had vanished – they almost trotted back to the farm.

'Look at those two,' moaned Jane, as they pulled her along the road. 'I've had to bully them all day and now they're pulling me off my feet.'

'That's because you're too soft with them,' retorted her father. He turned to Tom and nodded in the direction of the two lively mares. 'Just like women, Tom. If you're too soft, they'll take you for a ride!'

* * *

The new electric light hung from the farm ceiling, vying for space with the sides and hams which traditionally dominated the family table immediately below.

Edith conscientiously prodded her latest mat, while Esther, absorbed in a novel at the other corner of the table, finished her cup of coffee. Only the sound of crackling logs disturbed the peace of the room, a peace which didn't last.

'Come on in, Tom . . . you must be soaked. Have a seat over at that side of the fire. I'll make you a cup of coffee. I'm sure you're ready for one.'

'Aye,' agreed Jackson. 'It'll be a welcome drink after a hard day's work. Look at our Esther over there. She hasn't finished the cup of coffee she started half an hour ago. If we drank tea and coffee as often as these women do, we'd all be in debt by now.'

Tom laughed as he took off his jacket and gave it to Edith to dry by the fire.

'The only person who's likely to drink the profits in this family is just about to burn his clogs if he's not careful,' retorted Edith, placing mugs and cake on the nearest corner of the table.

Jackson obediently moved his clogs from the fireside and took them off. 'My God, Tom. Look at the corkers on that clog, they're about to drop off.'

He turned to his daughter who had hitherto ignored his remarks. 'Just look at these. If I sat around drinking coffee all day like some folk my corkers would be as good as new at the end of the year. . . Go and fetch me a hammer and a few nails, Esther. I'll have to mend this clog tonight if it's going to be fit to wear tomorrow.'

He turned in Tom's direction as Edith handed the two men a mug of coffee each with a piece of cake.

'If it fairs up tomorrow I'd like to get a bit more ploughing done, and I can't do that in bare feet. Somebody's got to be ready to do the work.'

'If it rains any more it'll be webbed feet you need, not clogs,' laughed Tom.

Esther handed her father a hammer and nails.

'Aye, at this time of year if it's not raining, it's freezing. Last week we snagged turnips for two days, and our fingers were so cold it would have been easy to cut a couple off without knowing owt about it.'

Jackson placed his clog, sole uppermost, between his knees as he spoke. Then he carefully positioned the nails between his lips.

'I've heard of that happening,' said Tom, enjoying his coffee.

'Mind you don't swallow those nails, Jackson,' warned Edith. 'They don't look safe to me, stuck in your mouth.'

'There's nothing to stop them going straight down,' laughed Esther. 'Dad has no teeth left, Mr Graham.'

'Yes he has,' said Edith coming to her silent husband's defence. 'He still has five.'

'Well, I've never seen them. They must be hiding somewhere at the back. Why don't you go to a dentist, Dad? He'll pull them out for you and fit you with a set of false teeth.'

'You can get dental treatment free now, Jackson,' nodded Tom in agreement.

Jackson took the nails out of his mouth, placed them on the corner of the table, and helped himself to a drink of coffee and a piece of cake, before replying.

'Dentist? I've never been to a dentist in my life. It was enough for me watching Martin Scott when he used to pull teeth in Egremont market place.'

'Who was he, Dad?'

'A dentist of course. They didn't have surgeries and white coats in those days. Anybody could pull teeth. When we were lads we used to go and watch.'

'I bet it hurt!' Esther was shocked at the thought.

'But so does toothache,' pointed out her mother. 'It was a case of which hurt most.'

'That's right. . .' Tom knocked his pipe out against the fireplace. 'Martin was very fast if it was an easy tooth.'

'A bit messy if it wasn't,' nodded Jackson.

'How did he know if he'd got the right tooth?' asked Mary.

'That was the patient's problem. Martin took out the one he was asked to pull. If the customer came back it would cost him the same again to have another one out.'

Tom chuckled as he recounted the tale. *His* memory also went back a good forty years before Esther's birth. 'You must remember, lass, there was no entertainment in those days – no picture house, no radio, no magazines. Tooth-pulling couldn't be missed! All us kids used to gather in the market place . . . it was rare entertainment.'

Jackson laughed at the memory. 'Tom's right – there wasn't much to amuse us when we were kids, not like there is now. . . Tom, do you remember Ken Black's pig? The clever little bugger charged us a halfpenny each to have a look at it!'

Tom laughed, then took up the story. 'We were going to school. We can't have been very old because we left when we were twelve or so in those days.'

'Only if you could pass the labour exam,' Edith explained to her astonished daughter.

Tom continued his tale. 'We had to pay for our schooling then – a halfpenny a week – and we had to buy our own slates.'

'That's right,' interrupted Jackson. 'We bought slate pencils . . . nothing so posh as paper and fountain pens. But we did well enough without much education. I've managed to pay my way all my life.'

'What about Ken whatever-his-name's pig?'

'Finish your story, Tom,' said Jackson, picking up the faulty clog.

'Ken Black's father kept a sow in a little hut at the bottom of his garden. On the Sunday night the hut had caught fire and it was well ablaze before Ken's dad smelled the burning wood . . . and pig!'

'How awful! Did the pig die? asked Esther, shocked at the thought.

'No it wasn't dead, but it was blackened.'

'A black . . . Large White!' Jackson had taken the nails from his mouth to chuckle at his own joke.

Tom continued his tale. 'Its skin was black and charred, its ears had nearly burnt off, and only a stump of tail was left. Ken's dad put up a few bits of wood to keep it in until he could build a new hut. Ken told the story on the way to school, so we asked him if we could come and look at his pig. . . But the crafty bugger asked us for our school money – a halfpenny for a look.'

'Dad, you didn't pay?'

'Of course we did.'

'What about school?'

'Well, what about school?' repeated her father. 'We managed without it that week! It was hot weather, so we spent most days on the beach.'

'Didn't the teacher write to your parents?'

Patiently Tom explained. 'In those days parents often couldn't read very well . . . and probably couldn't write at all, even if they had pen and paper.'

'Teachers weren't so good at it either,' added her father. 'But we learned enough to manage.'

Esther thought for a few minutes. 'Dad?'

'What do you want to know now? Can't a fella mend his clog in peace?'

'Did you ever have *your* teeth pulled out in the market place?'

'Not bloody likely! Think I'd make a fool of myself in front of the whole town?'

The two men laughed at Esther's concern.

'If you've only got five teeth left, who took the rest out?'

'Me.'

'How?'

'With a pair of scissors.'

'Good heavens! Didn't it hurt?'

'A bit. Most of them broke into bits, then I had to howk the roots out with a good pair of scissors. I never really had much bother after that.'

Esther was aghast at her father's revelation. 'How on earth do you manage to eat with only a few teeth?'

'No bother at all. I can eat anything – I have a grand set of gums.'

'That's right,' agreed Tom. 'Your father can eat more things than me, and I have a mouth full of dentures. I only went to please the missus. She said something about being smart and younger-looking. The trouble is I have to take them out to eat, and my gums never get really hard, so they're often sore. Your dad's sensible. False teeth are more trouble than they're worth.'

'If I got some false teeth I probably couldn't whistle the dog to round up the cows,' observed Jackson. 'Alan Steel has had a set for a few years now, but he has to put them in his pocket before he can manage his sheep. At first he tried to whistle with his new teeth in, but they flew out all over the spot. Even his dog learned to stand well back!'

His listeners laughed as they learned of one of Alan's less well-publicised embarrassments.

Tom watched as Jackson brought the hammer down sharply, securing the stray corkers.

'That's a good job done, Tom. I can walk a few miles in those tomorrow.'

He placed his clogs at the end of the fender, took his black twist from his pocket and slowly pared a piece with his penknife. 'Yes,' he continued, having placed a small piece of black tobacco on his tongue, 'my clogs'll last a good few miles – but I'm not so sure about Peggy's shoes. She's been rattling round the yard for the past week – but nobody seems to have noticed. If horses could talk they'd have to ask for every bloody thing they needed. Our Bill never seems to see if anything's wrong. The mare is only shod on the front feet anyway – that's not many to notice –

and he hasn't mentioned a thing. But I bet he'd soon shout if his own were slack.

Esther looked up from her book. 'Oh Dad, stop grumbling. I'll take her up to Mr Pearson first thing tomorrow morning while you're doing the milking. It won't take long.'

'Remember to take her by the back lonning then. You know how he likes her to walk through as much water and sludge as possible to soften her feet before she gets there.'

'Yes I know that, Dad. It makes it easier for him to cut and shape her feet. He's getting a bit frail now so I help him as much as I can – I think he finds cart horses' feet a bit heavy to lift now. But he likes Peggy, she's so quiet and well-behaved. Mind you, she always nuzzles his pocket. She knows which one has a few sweets in!'

'I never have my horses' back feet shod either and that helps – he's very nervous of doing back feet now.'

'You're right,' agreed Tom. 'I took that new black gelding of mine. He heard him walking up the road towards the smithy and he'd already made up his mind before we came into sight that four shoes were too much for him. But he did look him over, he likes to see all the new horses we get, especially any with a good pedigree.'

Jackson nodded approvingly. 'He's the best judge of horseflesh I know – and when he was younger he wouldn't have been nervous about tackling any horse's back feet. I've seen some right fights in his shop. Do you remember Dave Elliott who used to farm the other side of Beckermet? He bred some fine Shires.'

'Yes I do, Jackson. Daft sort of horses to expect to work in these little fields. They fall over their own feet when they turn in a narrow spot.'

'That's right. They have feet like huge mops, paddling about in the muck.'

'What were you going to say about Mr Pearson, Dad?'

At his daughter's prompting her father continued his reflections. 'I was remembering the fight Tim Pearson used to have with some of the Shires when Dave fetched them to be shod. Big white soft feet they had – he used to show them in the agricultural shows – so they had to be shod on all four feet. Great big clumsy horses they were. And by God, it takes some courage to pick up a young horse's leg, then start hammering the bloody daylights out of its foot . . . especially on its first visit!

Tom had relit his pipe while Jackson spoke. 'Often Tim would ask your dad or me to go along to help if Dave was bringing a young or difficult horse in to be shod.'

'What sort of help did Mr Pearson need?'

'Well, lass, if one of them big things kicks you hard you're not likely to be able to walk away. A blacksmith collected by a powerful back leg can travel a good distance – and can end up as a right mess, especially if he lands against the wall.'

'So what did you do?'

'Like a lot of blacksmiths, Tim used to have a block and tackle rigged up on a beam just above the doorway. A chain was fastened round the horse's hoof and it was hauled up and held still for him to work. Two or three men would hold the horse straight – the more help he had the easier it was.'

'Our Peggy would never be as badly behaved as that, even if we had her back feet shod.'

'Clydesdales can be as wicked in the blacksmith's as Shires, but horses that don't do much road work and have decent back feet only need their front feet shod.'

'That's right, Jackson. If you had to buy a new horse with only one consideration in mind, Esther, it would have to be because it had decent feet – good hard blue feet. Some show horses look smart with white feet and white legs, but they cut up like cheese.'

'Have you ever fancied breeding Shires, Dad?'

'Too big in every way, lass. They need bigger collars, bridles, hames – just you have a close look at the brewery horses next time you're in Whitehaven. *You'd* have a job to throw a saddle on their backs. And getting one of those big heavy collars over their heads is a real task for a lass – they can lift their heads up high and you'd not be able to reach high enough to harness it. No, give me a Clydesdale any day. They're strong, neat, good-natured work horses. . .'

Jackson paused for a moment, reflecting.

'I remember Jack Gordon, a neighbour, who farmed near Gosforth for a few years, before he went back down south. He had a bonny dappled grey Shire gelding. He was a grand worker and would pull anything anywhere, but he wouldn't let Jack put the collar over his head. He knew damn fine that Jack was just a little chap and a bit nervous of horses, so he deliberately lifted his head well out of reach.'

'What did Jack do?'

'He left its collar on – all the time . . . You remember him, Tom?'

'Aye, I've never seen anything like it. The stupid bugger used to graze with the collar dragging along the grass behind its head!'

'Then the bloody thing slept with the collar round its neck,' laughed Jackson. 'Now and again, if he managed to turn it round, the collar would slip off altogether. Then Jack had the trouble of getting it back on again. But, you know, he wasn't really a horseman – he couldn't cope if he bought a horse with any problems. And as for breeding . . . Well, he never even tried. He's one that'll make a good tractor man. Anyway he went back down south in the end. These hilly fields weren't his sort of farming.'

Tom refilled his pipe as he added his twopenn'orth. 'Yes, Esther. Breeding and breaking horses is a risky business. It's a darn sight easier to buy them after everybody else has done all the work.'

'Oh no!' exclaimed Esther. 'I would miss our yearly foal. The farm wouldn't be the same without one – they're beautiful.'

'That's the trouble with them,' said her father. 'We

know we can't keep them all. We just have to break them in, then sell them as useful working horses. That's economics for you. We've got to make a living – there's no room for sentiment in farming.'

'No room for sentiment?' retorted Edith. 'What about some of the things you've brought home from the auction? Remember that Dexter cow?'

She turned to Tom. 'You'll remember it, Tom. It was a bonny little cow . . . but it was so small its muck didn't drop into the usual drainge system so it made a mess in its stall. It had to be milked into a little calf bucket. It was unproductive, and a darn nuisance. . . '

Incensed by what he considered unfair criticism, Jackson tried to justify his impulse buy. 'Folk came from miles around to look at her. It gave them something to talk about in the pub . . . She came across from Ireland on one of them cattle boats that used to come regular to White-haven. She managed to swim ashore with the bigger beasts, so I thought she was worth a pound or two of my money.'

Esther joined the criticism. 'And what about that awful Chinese goose we once had? I was terrified of it, Mr Graham . . . When the geese were sitting hatching their eggs it wouldn't let me out of the house. It sat on its nest in the shed opposite the back door and flew at anybody who dared to come out! It had a horrible long neck and a vicious disposition. We only had it because no one else in the district had one . . . I know now why they got rid of it from China!'

Jackson looked scornfully at his daughter. 'Chinese or not, it knew you were frightened of it. All you had to do was to face up to it . . . it would soon have cleared off. It never chased me . . . It knew I would wring its bloody neck if it set its wicked eyes on me. But it was a very good layer and that's what matters, not what sort of manners it has.'

'Don't be silly, Jackson,' interrupted Edith. 'How could

she face up to it? She was only little then . . . We were all terrified of it. I must admit that I was only happy when it ended up on the Christmas table, even though it took you long enough to get round to killing it. I was beginning to think the two of you had developed a special friendship!'

'There's nothing like our own English breeds of geese and ducks . . .'

'Because they understand the language, I suppose!' laughed Tom.

'Talking about foreign breeds of duck, I thought I saw some of your Muscovies flying down by the river, Jackson.'

'If you did then they must be mine. No one else breeds any.'

'I know, they're not easy to breed – you seem to have a lot of luck with them.'

'Maybe, maybe,' agreed Jackson. 'But I'll not be able to

keep them much longer if the silly buggers keep flying down the beck.'

'Why's that, Jackson?'

'Well, yon stupid Alan Steel shot a couple of them last week!'

'What?'

'It's true enough. I was ploughing in the four acre down there by the beck when I heard the shots. He had them hanging on the side of his cart as I met him coming up the lonning.'

'Caught red-handed eh, Jackson?'

'Do you know he had the cheek to tell me he thought they were wild ducks!'

'What did you say to that?'

'I told him if they'd been wild ducks he would never have brought them down, he's too bad a shot! Anyway I took one and we ate it last Sunday.'

'What about the other one?'

'I told him to keep it. After all, it cost him enough in shot before he managed to hit two of them. Besides, it's time his wife had a taste of a decent bit of duck. Them skinny Scottish things he has running about his yard have practically no flesh on them. Even their eggs are poor – too small and not half as tasty as ours. Come to think of it, I'll have to clip their wings, or our ducks'll be laying their eggs in the beck, unless they get shot in flight first.'

'Here's a last cup of coffee,' said Edith, handing the cups around, 'and then it will be time for Tom to get away home. Mary will be wondering where he's got to.'

'It's a good thing Tom comes over to see us of an evening, Mother. Our Esther wouldn't learn a thing about real life if she had to rely on what education she gets from books . . . Drink up, Tom!'

8

MARKET DAY

'Look at your father, Esther – fast asleep! I wonder what he's dreaming about. He's twitched and mumbled in that chair since just after milking time.'

'He'll be tired, Mam. And, anyway, he'll need to be awake later. Tom's coming over to tell him how he's got on with his tatie round . . . You know how it brings back memories for Dad.'

'Oh yes, and it brings memories back for me as well. I also remember how long the Thursdays were before the war, when he had to set off before five o'clock in the morning to be there before the women started to shop, then make sure that one or two pubs were still in business on the way back!'

Edith would have been surprised had she known how close she was to what Jackson was reliving in his dream. . .

It was Wednesday night and the cart was almost loaded for tomorrow's journey to Whitehaven market. Jackson sighed as he looked over the load of potatoes, turnips, carrots and a few onions. That should do for this week. He had a few rabbits he could tie to the cart tomorrow morning, then all would be ready for yet another market day. He knew the ready cash they would bring in would amply recompense him for the long and often wet journey to Whitehaven.

Rain! Rain! Rain! He could feel it trying to find its way beneath his collar and up his trouser legs.

'Come on, Captain,' he urged as the powerful Shire breasted School House brow. The horse knew this was only the start of a tedious journey and he wasn't too keen to face the first of many hills. He shook his dripping mane in protest.

'You needn't try to wet me any more than I am already, you cantankerous bugger,' the old farmer observed.

Jackson usually walked up the hill to ease the load. He glanced down at the powerful animal's forefeet as they gripped the surface of the road. Rivulets of rainwater were splashing on to the ground to escape quickly back down the slope.

'We'll be swimming before long,' he remarked. At the summit Jackson allowed the horse a few minutes to catch its breath, then settled himself on the front of the cart to continue at a rattling rate past the sleeping Boonwood Hotel, and the equally quiet Golden Fleece in Calderbridge.

Jackson smiled to himself as he passed. In the very early morning the public houses, which had seemed so lively the previous evening, looked like lost ships or abandoned hulks floating on an unknown, uncharted sea.

'They won't be by this afternoon,' he thought as he traced his homeward journey in his mind's eye. Pubs were the returning farmer's milestones – unless, of course, you were a miserable bugger like Ezekiel Casson, one of the few farmers too religious even to cross the threshold of a pub. He remembered asking his mother years ago what the first Ezekiel had done . . . 'He was a prophet of gloom and doom,' she had said, 'who had a vision of God and some angels in a chariot.'

'Well,' mused Jackson, 'that fits. His wheels will be turning a bit nearer Whitehaven than mine are now.'

Egremont was awake as he went through – pitmen on their way to the ore mines, farmers on their way to the same market as himself. He called out to them, but they were too busy. They ignored him. 'I wonder why,' he mused.

Then he realised why – they weren't real people. They swarmed all over the town because they weren't people at all. They were worker ants!

Jackson wasn't surprised. Somehow he had expected it. He decided he would walk up the main street to restore feeling to his legs . . .

* * *

He shuffled in his sleep.

'He must be rounding up sheep or something – our Patch shuffles like that when he dozes,' laughed Esther.

'More likely he's reaching for another pint!' retorted Edith tartly.

At last Whitehaven came into view, the sea scarcely visible through the drizzle and pit smoke. 'Funny how Scotland has disappeared from the map,' thought Jackson. Well, it was only a matter of time. They've always wanted to be as far as possible from England. . . Maybe they'll join up with America. It's not that far away – they can float west with the wind if they're lucky.

'Downhill now, Captain. Then you can have a few hours rest, but not me. I've got to persuade them women down there that my taties are the best on the market,' he said to the weary horse.

Captain, Jackson and the loaded cart floated down towards the town and landed gently, like a huge seagull, in their usual place.

* * *

'Can't you knock a few pence off today? I'm one of your best customers, Mr Strong?'

'Do you think I'm made of money, Missus? I was digging these bloody taties all day yesterday, while you women were sitting with your feet up in front of a nice warm fire. . .'

'Warm fire? With coal the price it is these days!'

'Come on, lass. Your husband's like the rest of them who work down the pit – you're entitled to cheap coal. Miners don't have to fight with weather and wet rotting crops. They're nice and warm, without a drop of rain running down their backs. Good God, you don't know when you're well off.'

'I'd like to see you tell him to his face what a cushy job he has. . .'

'Don't take it to heart, Missus. I'll let you have one of these big cabbages for nowt, seeing that you come to my cart most Thursdays. Open your bag, lass.'

'I fancy one of them rabbits, Mr Strong. How long have they been dead?'

'Now then, Missus, you needn't worry about how fresh these are . . . I can tell you that they were both cocking their tails up at our dog yesterday morning . . . The little buggers had no idea it was Wednesday or they would have stopped in bed a bit longer! Just you have a close look at them, lass, and you can see the surprise is still written all over their faces.'

'Aye, well, you'd better be right or I'll buy from that miserable-faced chap down at the far end another time.'

'Ezekiel? Aye, you'll notice that his rabbits still have their paws crossed. He gives them time to say their prayers, then shoots them with his eyes shut. You can end up with lead shot anywhere from nose to tail. Here you are, along with a fat pumpkin to make the meal into something a bit special. And don't say you never get owt for nowt at this end of the market.'

'I didn't know local farmers grew pumpkins.'

'Oh yes, they grow well in my fields, and we breed fine strong mice in our buildings as well.'

'Fairy tales! You don't expect me to believe a word you say.'

Jackson was grateful when Percy Taylor, a friend from his pit days, came across from the pub with a glass of ale and something for him to eat – tripe, vinegar and a slice of raw onion wrapped in greaseproof paper.

'My God, these women are hard to please, Percy,' he said, settling himself on a shaft to eat.

'Times are hard for everybody, Jackson. These ladies have hardly any ready money to spend, so they must make as good a bargain as they can.'

'No. Shortage of money has nowt to do with it. They're women, that's all. They were made cussed and awkward – a thorn in a man's flesh, I think it says in the Bible.'

'When do you read the Bible? I though your reading was limited to fatstock prices!'

'No, I never read the Bible, Percy. I don't have time for such luxuries. I leave all that to Edith – she has the time and the inclination. Besides, I can't understand things that have two meanings. I like straightforward reading.'

'Well, just look at Zeke over there. You couldn't meet a more religious chap. He gets here long before the rest of you and sells out before you're half empty. He'll soon be off home . . . Now he's a fine example to the rest of you.'

'And I know he'll not stop at any pub on the way home like I do . . . Captain wouldn't know what had happened if we didn't stop at three pubs or more between here and Gosforth. But that grey mare of Zeke's never gets a minute's rest on the way back. And God knows what he does with all the time he's saved – he has no bloody idea how to enjoy himself!'

'Never mind. He'll probably have a good place reserved for him in the next world, Jackson.'

'Well, I'll just take one world at a time, Percy. And this one is bad enough, with women like some of these in Whitehaven to please.'

'I'm off now, you seem to have more customers heading this way.'

A tall woman with a hatchet-like face was bearing down on Jackson . . . Was she one of his customers?

Jackson wasn't sure.

The woman gathered speed, her clogs echoing across the marketplace and across the surrounding docks. . . The whole of Whitehaven paused to listen. She loomed above him now and the farmer could see that what he had thought were clogs were in fact two hoof-like feet!

'Look at this turnip I bought from you last week!'

A rotting mess was dripping from her claw-like fingers.

'I paid good money for this. I made a pact with you last Thursday . . . You said you could bet your life on the freshness of your turnip!' screamed the devilish woman. 'I've come to collect . . . your life.'

Jackson glanced around him, panicking. Only hard accusing eyes ringed his cart. The old farmer searched desperately for a friendly face.

In the far corner of the market he could just see Ezekiel moving off, but his back was turned and he was shaking his reins . . . As Jackson watched, the fiery wheels took off, climbing towards the heights of Hensingham.

'Zeke! Zeke! Come back and save me! I'll never say a bad word about you again. . . Just get rid of her. . . Zeke! Ezekiel!'

'My God! You took so much wakening, I reckoned you were dead!' laughed Tom as Edith successfully shook her husband back to wakefulness.

'You were shouting something about Ezekiel,' said Edith, 'so I knew you were going a long way back in time. He's been dead twenty years or more . . . A fine upstanding religious farmer he was, Tom.'

'He was that,' agreed Jackson warmly.

'It's a change to hear that from you, Jackson. You never had a good word to say for him when he was alive.'

'Maybe we get wiser as we get older, Edith. . . Yes, a fine man was Ezekiel Casson, one of the best.'

Tom had settled himself close to the warm fire. 'When I came home from my potato round I found Mary busy papering the parlour, so I thought it would be better if I cleared out of the way for a bit.'

'Aye, a good idea, Tom. I never like a woman under my feet if I'm doing anything important, so I expect they like to see the back of us as well if they're a bit on the busy side.'

Tom filled his pipe with a sigh of relief and leant back in the comfortable armchair just vacated by Edith.

'Thanks, Edith,' he said as she handed him a couple of pieces of cake, along with a mug of well-sugared tea. 'Just what a chap wants at the end of a busy day.'

Jackson spat expertly into the crackling flames . . . They did their best to spit back.

'Aye, it's a thankless job, Tom. Them Whitehaven women want to pay as little as possible. They never think of the hard work that's gone into all the produce on the cart.'

'Now, Jackson, when you worked in the pits you were the first to say that every penny you made was earned with blood and sweat,' pointed out Edith. And I shouldn't think those wives feel any differently.'

'Trust a woman to remember every word a man utters – when it suits her of course. But if I want a hand with a difficult calving or owt like that, she seems to be too far away to hear! It's a matter of priorities, Tom.'

'I wonder if Mary wanted any help,' Edith observed, glancing in Tom's direction. 'Men also seem to have a way of disappearing when we need a hand.'

'No, she didn't, Edith. She reckoned she was almost finished, and it would take her too long to show me how to match it up.'

'There you are!' said Jackson triumphantly. 'You women don't accept help when it's offered. There's Tom who's worked all day and comes home and offers to help his wife who's spent the day inside, warm and dry, while he's been trailing from door to door, begging folk to buy from him (folk who are too idle to carry a bit of shopping home) . . . That sort of husband is becoming a rarity nowadays!'

'You know as well as I do, Jackson, that since they built all those new housing estates in Whitehaven, and moved everybody out of the town centre, they've got to catch a bus into town and then queue to catch one back home again, lugging all their shopping and often a toddler or two as well . . . Town planners only plan for themselves. It's well seen that it's done by men who never have to struggle with shopping bags and small children.'

'Let's hope the day never comes when the town is planned by women, Tom. God knows what we'd end up with – rows of shops and no real amenities.'

'If, by "amenities", you mean pubs, billiard halls and men's toilets built almost on to the pavements, then you're right . . . It's time there were facilities for women in our towns.'

'Well, I'll be damned. . . You only have to go to any railway station and what do you see? Waiting rooms – for women only! What could be better than that, Edith? Waiting rooms with fires in as well – what more could you want?'

'Public toilets for women. It's a long way to the railway station to use a toilet, and pubs aren't the place for us. It seems to me that most towns were built with only men in mind.'

'Next time your Mary decides to paper the parlour you'd better walk on past our house, Tom, and drown your sorrows in the Grey Mare. You won't hear any daft talk about public closets for women there. We've only just managed to get them put into our houses, and that's been bad enough, without rearranging the whole of White-haven.

Tom nodded agreement.

'What sort of day have you had then, Tom? I wouldn't fancy selling taties like you do all around the estates. I prefer the market. It was bad enough delivering *milk* to folks' doorsteps. . .'

Edith shook her head in exasperation, remembering that it was she and not her husband who had delivered the milk in all weathers when they had had a milk round, but she knew it was useless to remind him of this. Giving other people credit had never been one of Jackson's strong points. She sighed.

'Haven't you anything useful to do, Edith, instead of waiting to contradict a chap every time he opens his mouth?' demanded Jackson, noticing her expression.

'It hasn't been a good day today, Jackson,' said Tom reflectively.

'Didn't you sell very much?'

'No, The reason was that last week I was short of a few taties. It had been too wet to get on the land, so I bought a few bags in from Alan Steel. They looked all right. . . But they must have been a bit strong or something because this week all the women were complaining, saying that if my taties were as bad as last week's then I needn't call again.'

'What on earth was wrong with Alan's taties then, Tom?' asked a concerned Edith, looking up from her sewing.

Jackson was already chuckling, his chair rocking under him. 'I might have known! The same thing happened to me years ago. . .!'

Edith looked alarmed. 'What did you do to your customers years ago, Jackson?'

'I did what I've seen Alan do. I thought if I put more manure on my crops they would grow bigger and tastier . . . and housewives are always looking for the biggest potatoes, thinking they're the best. Well, after I'd sold a cartload, off I went, pleased that I'd sold out before the rest.'

Tom smiled knowingly.

'But the next week, all hell was let loose in the marketplace. And remember, it was like being on a stage down there . . . Everybody within half a mile could hear these bloody women complaining about my taties. And think on, the place was packed with shoppers – no quiet words on the doorstep of one of these posh new, semi-detached houses. One woman said her family had had to use two *News of the Worlds* and a week's *Daily Heralds* in their new water closet!'

Tom nodded his head with feeling.

'I learned that lesson the hard way, just like you did this morning, Tom.'

'What did you say to them, Jackson?'

'What could I say? I explained that I'd put a generous load of hull muck on them to give them a good start, but it was nowt to worry about. A bit of belly ache is to be expected if you eat too many of my big taties with your Sunday dinner . . . It's a question of greed.'

'I wish I'd been there. I would have given them some potatoes for nothing to make up for it,' said Edith anxiously.

'We'd be in the workhouse if I let you interfere with the business side of things. You'd think we had money to throw away!'

'My God, some of these women are like tigers,' broke in Tom. 'No wonder I never see any husbands about the house when I call. I bet they daren't be off work for a day. Women like them take no prisoners, Jackson!'

Jackson was still laughing gleefully at Tom's predicament.

'It's easier to sell through a wholesaler, Tom. It's time to change over. It's getting worse facing the public these days, especially the women. A chap can't cope with more than one at a time, and he can manage that better if she's at home. Other men don't control their wives like we do out in the countryside. No, town life isn't for the likes of us, Tom.'

'It must have been hard years ago, Jackson.'

'We didn't know any other way . . . The horse was left in

a livery stable for sixpence, with its own feed. Then *I*, not the bloody horse, had to stand and sell in one spot all day. . . And if someone came into the market with a few plump rabbits (that had cost him nothing to breed), or had something extra hanging on his cart, your luck might be out that week. Women are faithless shoppers you know, Tom, especially when there's another dozen or so carts parked in the marketplace. And if they turn vicious, God help you.' He nodded in his wife's direction. 'And our Edith would have all the pubs and closets pulled down, so there'd be no escaping from them.'

'Since when did you leave your produce in the market while you went to sit in a pub?' There wouldn't have been much left when you returned to an unattended cart,' observed Edith quietly.

'You're right, I never did leave my cart. Luckily I had a good spot. Yes, Tom, it was a long hard day. Few could hide in a pub, unless they had a wife who would help them out.'

'If they had sold their butter and eggs in the butter market they might help their husbands. But most women had to do a bit of shopping for things they needed, like clothes and hardware. It was often a case of spending the money as soon as they got it, before their husbands drank it,' said Edith tartly.

'The things women say, Tom . . . You're condemned before you've committed a crime. Thank God women aren't magistrates. If that day ever arrives, marriage will be a thing of the past. Men won't dare get tied to a woman for life. It'll be as good as signing up for penal servitude!'

'One thing I reckon was unfair today was that I gave a turnip away free if the housewife bought a stone of potatoes and vegetables from me,' complained Tom. 'Most of them got one last week, but they don't seem to remember things like that. These taties have been my first mistake, one that anyone could have made, but they don't give you the benefit of the doubt. They were like a load of witches – after my blood!'

'But, Tom, you won't be daft enough to buy anything from the likes of Alan Steel a second time. Your mistake was in being too idle. You should have made sure you had enough potatoes stored in the barn just in case the weather was too bad . . . Once you have a tatie round, you've got to have what your customers want every week without fail or they'll drop you faster than a rotten egg. There's no justice, Tom. I can vouch for that!'

'I must pop over to your house tomorrow and see what sort of paper Mary has put up in her parlour,' mused Edith.

'I don't know why she papered it, Jackson,' said Tom. 'We only go in there on Christmas day and when there's a funeral in the family. I don't know why it needed doing up. I never see it, and if I ever land up in there for any length of time I won't be in a fit state to see what sort of pattern she picked anyway.'

'Who cares about you, Tom? You should know by now that parlours are for other folk to admire when they come to a laying out. According to Edith's sister, May, the entire reputation of the family is judged by what the callers think about the best room in the house. And they are supposed to be calling to pay their respects to the dead! No, Tom, you don't understand the idea at all. The gossip for the next ten years will be about Mary's choice of paper in the parlour.'

Jackson laughed at his own joke.

'There's a thought now, Tom! Is there a likelihood of anybody dying in the near future in your house? If it was me I'd be feeling a bit uneasy at this sort of activity . . .'

'Oh, Jackson, for goodness sake stop talking such a load of rubbish,' Edith reproved him. 'Tom has come round to talk about his day's work and you've been as unhelpful as you can possibly be.'

She turned to Tom. 'Your customers will have forgotten about the poor potatoes when they taste the ones they've bought today. Memories are short . . . Things will improve,

I'm sure of that. And as for papering, Mary has talked for a long time about spring-cleaning. We've all got to keep an eye on things or else the decorating will get away on us.'

Jackson looked suspiciously in Edith's direction. 'Spring-cleaning eh? More money to be spent on rooms that most of us don't know exist . . . Just on the offchance that a chap might break his neck, or eat a bellyful of rotten potatoes!' He laughed gleefully.

9

TORNADO

'I've never heard of such a thing happening up here before.'

'Nor anywhere else in England, Alan,' agreed Tom Graham as the drinkers in the Grey Mare nodded in acquiesence.

'They were saying that it was some sort of wrath from God,' volunteered Jean from behind the bar.

'Have you ever heard anything so daft?' retorted Jackson from his usual place close to the fire. 'If God wanted to pay us back for the sins we've committed He could have killed the lot of us . . . but nobody was killed, so I can't see how anybody can think that.'

'You should have seen the damage that was done in Egremont,' said Tom. 'Slates were blown over half a mile away and some houses lost their roofs.'

'And one of them prefabs was blown a good twenty feet down the road,' commented Alan Steel. 'Thank God the woman who lives there was staying with her daughter.'

'We take our good weather for granted,' said Jackson. 'In America, where our Jack lives, they have to put up with that sort of thing all the time.'

'Trust the Americans to have something worse than anything we can experience,' observed Jean from the bar.

'It's an everyday thing over there,' continued Jackson. 'They say that first the skies darken, with huge flocks of birds fleeing ahead of the storm. Then even the soil is swept up and carried away, along with the seeds the farmers have sown.'

'It must be hard to farm under those conditions,' said Alan. 'I thought men like your brother went to the States to earn a better living than they could here.'

'*They* thought the same thing, Alan. Most of them knew nothing about the terrible dust storms until they got settled in. Then it was a bit late to do anything . . . Mind you, a lot of them moved on to find more friendly places. And the ones that couldn't afford to move had to stay where they were and farm as best they could.'

'It must have been awful for the wives,' said Jean

'Typical of a woman's way of thnking,' retorted Jackson. 'They were safe enough most of the time. It was the men who had to decide whether to move on or stay. The trouble was, they couldn't have been wise farmers because they only had to look and see that the Indians weren't ploughing or sowing them prairies.'

'The Indians were primitive people though, Jackson,' laughed Alan. 'There was no history of them tilling the soil. They had probably never seen a plough!'

'That's what us civilised folk say. But the natives had always lived reasonably well, or else they would have all died out.'

'I suppose that makes sense,' agreed Tom.

'Some parts of the prairies had hailstones which lay to a depth of six inches, then drought which no irrigation system could put right. It would have cost too much . . . At least that's what our Jack wrote in his letters. You'd have to ask our Edith about it. She's the one who writes the letters in our house.'

'That's disgraceful, Jackson,' exclaimed Jean. 'He's *your* brother. You should do the writing.'

'Why do you think I married a lass who'd passed the Labour Exam, Jean? I don't believe in two folks doing the same job . . . Anyway, Jack reckoned the best thing to do was to leave the place to the Indians who could live off the wandering antelope and buffalo when the land was returned to grass plains. A darned sight easier than struggling with moving soil if you ask me.'

'Well, we can't return Egremont to any of them primitive tribes,' joked Alan. 'We have to rely on chaps like

112

you to make us feel that we didn't get such a bad deal with our own tornado last Wednesday . . . It could have been a lot worse if this had been America instead of England!'

'I reckon the Good Lord made a mistake,' said Jackson thoughtfully. 'It must be very easy for Him to get different parts of the world mixed up.'

'You mean the prayers manage to cross lines.'

'That's right Jean. Now you said it might be the wrath of God, but when I read about it in the *Whitehaven News* I noticed that the Manse was almost destroyed. Surely He wouldn't want to make the folk who are on His side homeless?'

'But in the Old Testament He destroyed most of the world with the Great Flood. They couldn't all have been guilty, could they? And this was a bit like the Flood . . . The noise was terrifying. Folk in Egremont thought the end of the world had come.'

'Rubbish, Jean. People have too much imagination.'

'Didn't you hear it then, Jackson? It passed close to your house.'

'I go to bed to sleep, Tom.'

'I bet you wouldn't be so offhand if it had hit your farm and stripped the roof off like it did John's down the road there.'

'His farm was built way back in the sixteenth century or some such time – it's a wonder it's stood this long. Some of these wealthy landlords expect the bloody buildings to last for a thousand years or so. It takes a tornado to get them to put their hands in their pockets to bring their property up to date!'

'The worst thing for me was the electricity being cut off,' declared Alan Steel. 'A lot of farmers had to wait most of the day before they could milk.'

'Serves you right for buying too many cows when you hadn't to milk by hand any more. Greed, that's what it is. You over-graze your fields, then you have to spend more money on fancy, expensive fertilisers. And in the end if there's no electricity you can't manage to milk the cows by hand. I've been careful not to buy too many milk cows. There's nothing to beat a good mixed farm.'

'The folk who were homeless had to spend the night in the Red Lion,' announced Jean.

'It would do most of them good to see the inside of a pub,' laughed Jackson. 'A lot of women seem to think a pub is just a spot where their husband wastes his well-earned spare time. Spending a few nights in one will widen their outlook a bit. And they may have noticed that the pubs were left standing . . . That's something to think about, isn't it? Maybe some of these religious folk who are against drink have got it all wrong. You can interpret these balls of fire from heaven in different ways! And who's to say who's right?'

'Trust you to see things that way,' laughed Tom. 'Maybe you should ask your Edith what she thinks?'

'She's like a few more, she'll ask the vicar or the priest for an explanation . . . somebody like that chap from the Manse who's spending this week under a strange roof!'

*　*　*

Jackson leant thoughtfully on the field gate, considering the stirks grazing contentedly in the meadow. The warm summer evening wrapped itself gently around him as he assessed the young stock.

'You seem to be far away, Jackson!' a familiar voice startled him.

'I was just looking at the colours of the young stock I've got in this field, Tom. At one time they were all Short-horns, with a smattering of other breeds. But now I can have any sort of breed grazing side by side . . . The AI have certainly brought a change to farming.'

'Yes, you're right, Jackson. But the way things are going, soon they'll all be black and white. Only the Friesians seem to produce the quality of milk we require these days.'

'That's a shame, Tom. It'll be hard to know which cow is which when they all look the same. But I suppose we've got to move with the times. We're in it for the money when all's said and done.'

'That's not like you to say that, Jackson. You've always reckoned that a real farmer is in it for the pleasure of breeding fine stock and growing good food for the country.'

'A chap can think two things at once you know, Tom. It's a case of keeping an open mind as the times change. Besides, I'm not always sure that my original ideas are wrong . . . It's a question of waiting to see.'

'Why? Is something wrong with them stirks? They look OK to me.'

'Just you look a bit more closely at yon Hereford cross. I've never kept many Herefords, but that heifer hasn't looked right since the day she was born. Them AI vets could be fobbing me off with sub-standard stuff . . . I always knew if our bull was off-colour and needed a bit of extra feed to keep him in condition, but I have no idea what sort of condition their bulls are in.' Jackson shook his head sadly. 'No, with these new-fangled things you have to take a lot on trust.'

'Aye, that heifer does look a bit sad and sorry for herself, now you come to mention it. But you could have had a weak one from your own bull.'

Jackson was obviously not convinced. 'Anyhow, when the vet comes again I'll let him have a look at her. Maybe he can give me a reduced rate on the next insemination. After all, it should be payment by results. Yes, that's what I'll do, Tom.'

Tom laughed. 'Come on, Jackson. You can't blame a poor crop on the weather, then ask the Lord to pay you some compensation because He didn't deliver the sun on the days best suited to you. This is the same sort of thing – you have to take a chance. The vet might reckon that you haven't looked after it as well as the others. You have no complaints about the rest of them so the fault could be in your cow.'

Jackson's eyebrows shot up. 'I hardly think so. All Rose's other calves were healthy enough, and most of them were heifers. But I can't say we've had as many heifers with this new AI as we did with our own bulls. They seemed to know how to produce the heifers we want.'

'How many calves has she had?'

'Let me see now . . . It must be a good ten or so, and every one a beauty.'

'Maybe it's time you pensioned her off then.'

'No, no. I've had plenty of cows that have had more calves than Rose, and she's still a fine milker. No, she's the product of good farming, Tom. I'll have to search some-where else for the fault. Just look at the bloody little bugger – it's the only one to have laid down while all the rest are eating. A half-hearted thing if ever there was one! I'll have a job to fatten it up for beef. I daren't keep it to milk. It'll only breed more weaklings like itself and will be half-hearted about producing milk.'

Jackson rattled his stick sharply against the gate to encourage the heifer to stand up and graze. She did, with alacrity, as though sensing her owner's annoyance at her slow rate of growth. 'That's better, you lazy bugger. You can at least fatten yourself up.'

He turned to Tom. 'You'd think our Esther had been talking to the calf. She's on a diet, or so she tells me. I can't think why she's decided to eat less now when I've spent good money on her for so many years. She should have decided to eat as little as possible when times were hard . . . There's no understanding these young lasses.'

'You know, I've been thinking, Jackson . . .'

'About our Esther hungering herself?'

'No, about when that heifer was born. Wasn't it early on in the year?'

'Aye, it was – about the middle of January. What's that got to do with her condition?'

'But don't you remember, Jackson? Wasn't that about the time of the tornado?'

'By God you're right, Tom. She was born on 17th January . . . I remember saying to our Edith that Rose had had her calf that night. But Rose never bothers herself about anything. She is the least troublesome of all our cows.'

'Well, you never know, Jackson. The poor beast can't talk, and you have a habit of putting words in your animals' mouths. She was probably terrified and wasn't intending to calve at all that night.'

'I never gave it a thought, Tom. You might just be right. The old farmers used to say that unusual happenings could cause cows to drop poor calves. I didn't believe them, because most of them were a pack of liars anyway, but you never know . . . There could be a bit of truth in it.'

As Tom made his way in the direction of his own farm, Jackson had another look at his heifer. 'A load of superstitious nonsense! It would take more than a tornado to make Rose part with her calf before time. It's the bloody bull that's at fault . . . But I'd better not mention a word about tornadoes to Edith or she'll say it's the wrath of God or some such bloody daft thing. It's better if I let them all think they're right. That way I'll please the lot of them.'

He chuckled to himself as he made his way back to the farmhouse. 'What a chap has to do to keep the peace with everybody! But farming has always been a gamble and perhaps it's better to cross neither the Lord nor the Devil, just in case . . .'

10

A FLYING HORSE

'You're late in tonight, Jackson. I saw you ploughing with that new black mare you bought last
week. It's not like you to buy another mare.
You're always saying that we all keep too many mares and
have nothing to work with when they foal in spring.'

'Evening, Alan!' Jackson nodded at his questioner.
'Can't a chap find a decent seat before he has to answer a
daft question?'

'There's a drink in for you,' smiled Jean. 'One of them
atom workers left it for you. I think he enjoyed the crack
last week.'

'Point him out to me will you, Jean, when he comes in
next, and I'll thank him. It's well seen that they have
money to burn down there.'

'We thought the same thing when we saw that black
mare working with Peggy,' said one of the younger
drinkers. 'We can't make out why you bought a Shire
cross.'

Jackson lowered his drink slowly and reflectively. 'The
trouble with you young chaps, who have had money and a
good farm handed on to you, is that you think a mare is
only used for breeding, and does a bit of light work on the
side in the spring.'

Alan nodded in agreement. 'That's why we find a strong
mare useful – at last a miner chap like you is beginning to
pick up a few things from us real farmers!'

A murmur ran around the bar. Jackson wouldn't take
such a comment lying down.

The farmer drew his chair closer to the pub fire. His dog
Patch shuffled along underneath, too weary to lift his belly

off the large blue flagstones, glad to creep closer to the glowing embers on such a cold night.

'You know Alan . . .' he began patiently, 'if you had a litter of poor, weak pigs you wouldn't decide to breed from them, would you?'

'No, that stands to reason – but that mare looks a reasonable animal.'

'Maybe . . . But my point is that just because she happens to be a mare it doesn't mean I've bought her to breed.'

Abe Mossop, who'd been listening from the domino table, laughed as he interrupted the conversation. 'If you don't want to breed from her then why didn't you buy a strong gelding? I heard there were some fine-looking ones in the sale you went to last week.'

'Aye,' agreed Alan. 'I was there and I saw you standing with your hands in your pockets while they walked some useful-looking geldings around the ring – years of work in them.'

Jackson listened patiently to each of his friends as they spoke, and nodded. 'Yes, you're right,' he answered slowly. 'But if you think back, you'll also remember that those fine, strong, well-bred horses were going for well over £100 . . . I don't have that sort of money in *my* pocket. A few years back I paid out good money that I could ill-afford for Peggy – I was dazzled by a smart-looking filly with a long pedigree. So now I have the sense to keep my money in my pocket and let a tempting buy walk past.'

'So what made you buy an unsuitable mare then?' asked Joe Watson the shopkeeper.

'Well Joe, it's a bit like you shopkeepers selling those ugly whalebone stays to fat women.'

The assembled farmers started to laugh.

'What have whalebone stays got to do with buying a horse, Jackson? God knows what tale he is going to tell us now,' laughed Tom Graham who'd been sitting silently at the domino table during his friend's speech.

'It's a question of what you put in the shop window, Tom, to attract the customer in. Then, when they realise the fancy clothes won't fit, you can sell them the ugly stays . . . They think that'll do the trick.'

'Explain a bit more,' urged a sceptical Alan.

'It's very tempting to buy a good-looking horse to parade up and down your fields . . .' Jackson spat expertly into the dancing flames before continuing. 'But then you find you have nowt left in your pocket to buy a friend a drink or to keep a couple of expensive daughters fed and clothed . . . No, Alan, I've got to resist the shop window and buy the stays.'

'What did you pay for the mare then?' asked Abe innocently. 'I agree she's a bit ugly. She doesn't seem too sure if she's a Shire or a Clydesdale.'

'Never you mind!' retorted the old farmer, reaching for his drink. 'I noticed that none of you rich farmers waited until the cheap horses – the ones with no character – were put up for sale.'

'Who wants to pay good money for trouble?' demanded Alan.

'Them that can't afford owt better,' replied Jackson tartly. 'A good strong mare like Jewel has years of work in her.'

'Jewel! Jewel!' How did a rough-looking cross-breed like that come by a name like Jewel?'

'Our Esther called her that ... As usual, the owner couldn't be found, not even in the pub – so we had to give her a name. We hardly ever have a black horse and Esther said something about her coat shining like a jewel, so that's what we called her. She seems to like everything we've asked her to do so far.'

'Come on, come on, Jackson. A horse sold without a character can't like everything. Does she bite, kick, refuse to to be harnessed? You must have found out by now,' coaxed Alan.

'She was working well with Peggy this afternoon when I looked across from our ten acre,' said Tom, hoping to save his friend any further embarrassment.

'That's nothing to go by,' snapped Alan. 'I don't think any new horse would dare to misbehave tied to Peggy – she wouldn't allow such a thing!'

He turned to Jackson. 'What's she like in the cart?'

Jackson shuffled uneasily in his chair and glanced enviously towards the domino players.

'Now we're getting to the truth!'

'She was cheap, I can't expect a lot of good manners from her.'

'She's turned out to be a wicked bugger then?'

'Not exactly, Abe, not exactly. She's just short of a bit of patient teaching, that's all.'

Alan Steel ordered another round from the interested Jean. 'Poor animal,' she said sympathetically. 'Some of these farmers talk about "breaking in" horses when they mean that they've broken the poor thing's heart.'

'Don't talk so daft!' said Alan scornfully. 'You women are too soft. You know nothing at all about training young animals – if you're not in control of them they'll soon be in control of you!'

'The lass is quite right,' interrupted Jackson. 'Every horse has a different temperament and has to be understood. That's why home-bred horses are best. Like one of the family, you get to know all their little ways.' He paused to drink his pint of Bitter. 'It's all the fault of these dealers who buy and sell young horses, making a profit at the expense of the animals . . . Then somebody like me has to sort it all out.'

'We still don't know what sort of fast trick this "jewel" of a mare has pulled on you,' persisted Alan Steel, determined not to let the old farmer off the hook.

Jackson could see that time was running out. Whatever happened – even in the privacy of his own farmyard – would soon be common knowledge. ('You'd think the bloody horses gossiped among themselves, let alone the farmers' he thought to himself.)

'Just a little problem, Alan . . . I never expected a perfect animal for the price I paid.'

An expectant silence fell on the group round the fire. They knew that any wickedness this new horse harboured would be the subject of comment and speculation for months if not years, especially if Jackson had managed to save a few pounds only to find that he had a completely unmanageable horse eating its head off at his expense.

Alan was impatient for the ammunition to fall into his lap.

'Well,' began Jackson reluctantly, 'there's nothing wrong that patience and kindness won't cure . . .'

'Good God, Jackson. Tell us what's wrong with the damn mare,' Alan exploded.

'A little uneasy, that's all, a little uneasy . . . A game of dominoes now . . .'

'Uneasy! When?' Alan pressed his quesion.

'She doesn't like a heavy saddle on her back . . .'

'You mean she won't take a load? A fat lot of use a mare like that will be. I reckon you'll have to settle for a few cross-bred foals from her. If they don't take after their mother they'll probably turn out all right.'

'She did accept a load, but refused to move off with it, just stood there – frozen – like Lot's wife. Not a foot could we persuade her to move. Bill had to unload her while I started milking.'

'A bloody useless horse to have about the place at hay and harvest time, Jackson. If she'll only work in chains she'll be like a tourist that comes to St Bees for the summer – idling about in the sun, then working hard in the winter! I reckon you've got a bargain there, seeing we only have three months of heavy carting all year!'

Jackson knew he could do little to salvage his reputation as a buyer of horseflesh on this particular evening . . . He would have to bide his time – opportunities always presented themselves eventually.

'Aye,' he nodded philosophically, 'this won't be the first awkward mare I've had to teach manners to . . . She has her good points though – our Jane was brushing her down when I left home and she reckons she has a lovely healthy coat. She'll put her in the paddock behind the house when she's finished. It'll be the first night we've put her outside with the other horses. She'll leave a head collar on her in case she's bad to catch in the morning.'

He paused, then rounded off his observations with panache. 'Yes, these wicked buggers soon find that I know all the tricks of the trade.'

He was about to make his way to the domino table when the pub door opened and Bill Brown stepped in, almost bumping into Jackson in his haste.

'This is where you are then, Jackson,' he greeted the old man warmly.

'Am I supposed to be in a better place?'

'You might have been of more use at home earlier in the evening, chasing that new mare of yours!'

'What do you mean, chasing his new mare?' asked a more than interested Alan Steel.

'Well, I've just passed your Jane – on the Braystones road . . .'

'What on earth is she doing there?' asked an alarmed Jackson.

'Pushing a bike and leading that new black mare at the same time.'

Jackson's anxiety turned to anger as soon as he knew that his daughter was fit and well. 'What the hell's been happening? I daren't go for a quiet pint without the stock being left to wander the length and breadth of the countryside!'

He sat down quickly in the nearest empty chair as an eager Alan Steel pursued his questioning.

'Tell us what happened,' he asked Bill encouragingly.

'When I pulled up alongside her, Jane said that she'd put the mare in the back field as her dad told her to . . .'

'At least she got that bit right,' snarled Jackson.'

'The mare was delighted to be free,' continued Bill. 'Off she went at full gallop down the paddock, but instead of turning round at the bottom and galloping round the edge of the field, she jumped the little beck near the bottom. Then, instead of slowing down, she gathered speed and cleared Tom's hedge – with room to spare! She disappeared in the direction of Braystones without a backward glance.'

'What on earth did Jane do?' asked an astonished Joe Watson.

'Went by road on her bike, hoping to head the horse off if it crossed the road.'

'It beats me how a heavy Shire like that can jump heights,' exclaimed Tom. 'She has feet like floor mops!'

'She must look like an Old English sheepdog flying through the air with all the loose hair she has on her,' laughed a delighted Alan Steel.

The entire crowd chuckled at this unfortunate turn of events for Jackson. Bill Brown continued his account of the evening, pleased to be the centre of attention for once, and even more pleased that he knew more than Jackson did about the drama that had taken place on his own farm.

'It was miles before Jane caught up with the horse. The whole countryside had come alive with cows bellowing (some thought it was milking time). Some young stock were just galloping about to keep the flying horse company. A few dogs chased her but she soon left them behind – they weren't so keen to clear gates and hedges . . . You've missed all the fun, Jackson!'

Jackson had once again risen to his feet and was making his way to the door, anxious to find out about the goings-on at home, and even more anxious to escape the jibes of the delighted drinkers. 'If she won't take more than ten stone on her back by next spring, Jackson, you can always enter her for the Grand National!' called Alan to the closing door.

11

SEA FOOD

The heavy, lumbering animals swayed clumsily as they crossed and recrossed the road to graze the tasty verges of the country road. A spell on each verge satisfied them that the long grass was as tasty on either side.

Jackson followed slowly behind, content to pause and let the cows eat the grass which they normally had to pass by. He had fetched them an hour earlier than usual so they could trail home slowly, eating as they went.

'There's that bloody Nancy bullying the other cows again,' he said to himself. 'They daren't reach for a tasty bite anywhere near her, or she gets her wicked horns stuck in their sides. But that's all part of nature I suppose – the strong survive at the expense of the weak. Human beings have always done the same thing, but they are cleverer and wickeder with it.'

The sun baked his back pleasantly. Fresh grass along the dykes was a treat for his cows and the slow pace allowed their milk to reach the byre with the least possible pre-milking disturbance. Jackson settled himself on a low stone in the warm dyke-back, placed his stick close by, then took his chewing tobacco from his pocket. Patch stretched himself out on the smooth tarmac.

Any cars that might happen along could easily be driven between the lines of the cows which were grazing happily, noses to the side and backsides to the middle. Jackson appraised his herd as he sat contentedly chewing his black twist.

The whole countryside dozed in the sunshine, as though catching its breath before the frantic days of haymaking set the air buzzing with sounds of cutting, leading hay and men's voices shouting from field to field. Jackson knew that both hay and corn were growing in the fields behind him, soaking up encouragement from the sun in order to produce a decent yield for the waiting farmers.

The cows were cleaning the grass very efficiently from the dykes, saving Jackson and his neighbours a bit of work when it came to dressing back the overgrowth. Besides, it was a shame to waste the good long grass simply because it grew on the roadside.

'You must have little work to do, Jackson, if you can waste time dozing in the dyke-backs while your beasts graze their own way home. Have you no grass left in that station field of yours?'

Jackson looked up in surprise. He hadn't noticed the cyclist approaching him – he must have dozed off.

'Hello, Jack!' he said companionably.

The cyclist dismounted, then propped his cycle in a nearby gateway.

'You have some fine plaice hanging there,' said Jackson, nodding in the direction of the loaded bicycle.

'Aye, I've been lucky today. I'll leave you one or two of whatever Edith fancies when I pass your gate.'

'Thanks, Jack. You know, to me, set lines are the only sensible way to catch fish. Them river fishing chaps seem to make things as difficult as they can, instead of letting nature and the tide do the work for them like clever men have done over the centuries.'

'You're right, Jackson. The garth down there at Nethertown must have been first dug a long time ago, maybe in the Middle Ages. After all, they had to live as best they could . . . There were no potatoes in those days so their diet must have been very limited.'

'I didn't know you were that well-educated, Jack. It's hard to imagine a time when there were no chips to go with the fish!'

'Some folk these days would have a hard time of it if

they couldn't make a plate of chips. And you should be thankful for that, Jackson. You would have a job to make ends meet if you had no taties to sell.'

'I would that, lad. Folk would have starved to death very easily in the Middle Ages if it hadn't been for the fish and the corn crops. I remember our Edith saying that the Irish potato famine was because the taties had rotted in the fields and they had nothing else to live on.'

'That's right. I like to read a bit of history, and we have a lot to be thankful for these days. I just wish someone would invent a fork to help me dig lugworms a bit better. The crafty little buggers seem to hear me walking over the sand and wriggle off as fast as they can.'

'It's them big heavy waders you all wear – a chap in bare feet could take them by surprise . . . Aye, we tend to think we've thought of all the clever things ourselves, but they must have been very smart to survive in them days.'

'Yes, Jackson. Take building a garth, for example . . . They had to choose a naturally good spot, then dig and make up the wicker sides. It had to be pretty deep to hold enough fish to feed the coastal villages. Think of it – fresh fish every day if you were lucky.'

'I suppose our ancestors ate well along this coastal strip, since they had the sea and the river to provide fish and the coastal plain was always fertile enough to be tilled. No wonder there are so many folk living on this coast.'

'I suppose you're right, Jackson. The only thing they didn't get in those days was the coal thrown from the engines. I watched this afternoon as the engine driver on the three o'clock train from Barrow shovelled coal out of his cab down to the beach bungalows. The folk that live below the track don't just wave to say hello!'

'Serves the railway company right, Jack. The amount of coal they use on this run would make any thinking person reckon that it was uphill all the way from Barrow to Carlisle.'

Jack laughed at his friend's assessment of the situation. 'Well, I'll have to move on, or the fish'll be stinking before it arrives in Egremont . . . Oh, by the way, Tommy from Whitehaven wants to know if Bill would like to go out fishing with him on Sunday morning off Nethertown?'

'I'm sure he'll want to go. What time should I tell him to be down there?'

'Eleven o'clock.'

'A sensible time of day, after the milking's done. I bet he'll get out of bed a darn sight quicker than he usually does so he can get to Nethertown in good time.'

Jackson watched as Jack carefully rode his loaded cycle between the distant cows. 'Well, if we don't get a move on, Patch, the cows'll be turning round and making their way back to meet us, thinking that milking time's over.'

Patch glanced up as his name was mentioned but, hearing no further command, trotted ahead, sniffing through the overpowering smell of cows for the more tempting scent of rabbits and voles. For him, this warm afternoon was a time to catch up on some sleep before the messy evening's herding. Why did cows lift their tails as they came out from milking? Sheep, to Patch, semed more sensible. At least they didn't stand above you, letting every part of their bodies swing in your direction!

He sighed for his lost life in the fells, but his reverie came to an abrupt end as his master's whistle and command reached his ears.

'Patch, how long is it going to take you to fetch that stupid bloody Mollie out of that lonning? She's halfway to Mother Bragg's cottage. She'll probably land back with a bicycle wheel stuck in her horns again!'

Patch raced to retrieve the offending cow. That one cow was more trouble than all the rest put together. She needed a dog all to herself.

'Patch is getting a bit old for this job. A new young dog would smarten some of these lazy cows up. They've got the measure of the old one and think they can do as they like,' Jackson muttered to himself, as the recalcitrant cow rejoined the herd. 'It's time I went up to Wasdale to see if Ben has a decent dog he's finished with – one that's a bit too old for the fells.'

* * *

Bill and his friend Tommy waited until the incoming tide brushed the shingle, then they pushed the small boat with its outboard motor expertly on to the lifting tide.

The beach was already fairly crowded with families who had walked the three miles or so from Egremont to spend the day by the sea. Many folk were sitting in front of the row of beach bungalows to watch the boat being launched. Each bungalow had a small front garden from where the lucky occupants could watch events on the shore. Some sold snacks and provided hot water for tea. On a sunny Sunday like this there was no better place to be. Bill felt excitement mount as the crowd of children waved them off.

Soon they were a fair distance from the shore, with Tommy manning the outboard motor. The sound of the playing, splashing children was barely audible now, as a calmness unknown to the land-locked settled around them. They could hear the gentle swell slapping softly against the side of the boat as Tommy cut the engine to allow them to prepare their lines. Thankfully the fumes drifted away, along with the noise of the motor.

The trailing lines disappeared through the translucent water, down to the lower depths where shoals of unsuspecting mackerel swam in military formation, in search of small fry. Their lines were hooked and baited with any shiny object that came to hand – silver paper, feathers or simply a bare hook. The engine was then restarted, allowing the boat to move off very slowly, the lines feeding out to trail hopefully in their wake.

Mackerel swim in large shoals, chasing glittering fry. Any lure which mimicked the tempting flash of the tiny fish would be sure to reap a gleaming harvest for the fishers.

'Are mackerel the only fish we're likely to catch today?' asked Bill eagerly.

'Maybe,' answered his friend, 'but we might be lucky enough to land a sea trout destined for the river over there, or a sea bass – which makes a tasty meal. Along this coast there are many species of fish, each one requiring a different angling technique. No one method works for every type unfortunately. But you know, Bill, even an inexperienced fisherman can be lucky and catch fish with no skill and unlikely bait. I once heard about a lad from Frizington who was fishing on the pier at Whitehaven, using a pickled onion as bait. The man sitting next to him asked why he was using such daft bait. "A fella who lives near us told me to try a pickled onion," he replied. Of course the fisherman knew that someone was having a joke at the youth's expense, so he filled the lad's bag with a few fine codfish and sent him back home to show what he had caught with his pickled onions . . . They reckoned the next day a couple of chaps from Frizington were to be seen hopefully fishing on the pier, their lines baited with . . . pickled onions!'

Bill laughed. He enjoyed this sort of fishing. Like his father, he wasn't one to spend time and money chasing fish which had already learned how to outwit all but the most expert of anglers. Sea fish seemed to be unversed in the devious ways of men – thank God.

He felt a tug on one line and began to haul it in, the motor still ticking over. He eased the hooks over the edge of the boat. What he had thought was a very big fish turned out to be three small ones. He could see them as they rose towards the surface. They gleamed and glinted in the water, flashing silver, blue and just a tinge of aqua-marine.

The thrashing fish thumped on to the bottom of the boat as Bill removed the hooks from their mouths.

'I think we've hit a shoal.' called Tommy, reaching for his line.

The boat circled the area slowly, as the two friends drew the fish in. Only an hour or so and they would have to make their way back to the shore or else the tide would be too far out for them to drag the boat easily above the high-tide mark.

Bill hardly felt the sun burning his face, he was so busy hauling, hooking and gutting their catch. Meanwhile, an attendant crowd of greedy screeching seagulls scooped an easy meal behind the boat.

At last they wound in their line and surveyed the fish box, brimming over with their catch.

'I reckon there's about forty to fifty in that box,' said Tommy happily. 'I think we'd better make our way back while we can still land the boat easily.'

He opened the throttle and the boat began to travel back towards the playing children and the racing dogs.

Bill's eyes rested for the first time that day on the patchwork of fields and farms dotting the coastal plain which rose out of the sea and shelved upwards to merge into the distant sun-speckled fells. He could see his father's fields basking in the warmth, taking their Sunday rest before the haytiming which would occupy the next few weeks.

A bluish heat haze curtained the outline of St Bees Head to his left, while the darker bulk of Black Combe watched over the Sunday activity from the south, the thread-like railway track linking the two. As his eye followed the track back northwards, he spotted a train pulling away from the Lilliputian station to snake its way gingerly along the face of the coastal cliff.

'I bet it's hot in that cab,' said Tommy, as though reading Bill's mind. 'I wouldn't like to be shovelling coal on a day like this. I wonder if he's looking out here and wishing to God that he was sitting with us.'

The noise from the waiting crowds now grew louder and Tommy had to watch out for eager swimmers who were racing to meet the boat.

'Look at them all, Bill. I can even see that woman with a big frying pan in her hand – as usual. She likes to make sure she gets a good panful for her supper. You'd think we'd gone out specially to keep all the folk on the beach in fish for the whole of next week!'

'I suppose we did, in a way. There's nothing like a warm welcome when you get ashore – and we'll have plenty of help to pull the boat up the beach.'

The children swarmed around the small boat as soon as it reached the shallows. Tommy and Bill handed out fish good-naturedly, knowing there would be plenty left for their own families and neighbours.

* * *

As soon as Bill stepped through the kitchen doorway he was aware of excited laughter.

'Look, Bill,' called Esther. 'Come and see our new dog. Dad's been up to Wasdale with Tom this afternoon and brought this lovely little dog back.'

Bill saw the nervous animal eagerly feeding from a dish under the table. She looked up warily as the newcomer approached.

'It's unusual for you to choose a white dog, Dad. I thought white was a bad colour – and I didn't know we needed a new dog.'

'The cows get far too much of their own way with Patch. A quick new dog will brighten their ideas up.'

'The trouble is that the cows are older than the dog and know a darn sight more than he does! I reckon you should get rid of the cows and buy some that'll give a bit more milk. It's our herd that needs updating if you ask me.'

'I wouldn't think of asking you, lad, because I know that most of your ideas come from that Young Farmers' Club you've joined. The day you can come up with a new idea that's your own I'll maybe listen. This little bitch has worked hard up in the fells but is getting a little slow now and should just do us nicely after she's had a bit of tuition with cows.'

'What's her name?'

'Flash,' answered his sister, as she coaxed the shy little dog to take a biscuit.

'The way you're spoiling her, we'll be lucky to get any work out of her,' grumbled Jackson. 'Leave her alone or it'll take me until dinnertime tomorrow to persuade her that she's come here to work.'

'But she's frightened, Dad. I want her to feel at home.'

'She's used to sleeping outside in the barn, so the best thing you can do is take her into the barn and leave her, instead of upsetting her with all this noise and fuss. It's enough to make her run back home if she gets half a chance.'

'Surely she won't do that?'

'I've known many a dog that's run back home when it's been sold – and all because somebody didn't give it a minute's peace! You don't fuss Patch like that, so leave the little lass alone until she finds her feet.'

'Just look at the mess your chest is, Bill!' gasped Edith, as Bill sat down painfully at the table for his tea. 'You shouldn't have taken your shirt off in a boat on such a hot day.'

'Serves him right if he's daft enought to sit and burn himself, Edith. Some folk have to learn the hard way.'

'A bit of sunburn is nothing,' insisted Bill. 'I enjoyed the day and you'll not say no to a bit of fresh fish if I know you, Dad!'

'If the mackerel are owt like them plaice Jack caught last week they'll do me fine.'

'Yes,' agreed Edith warmly. 'Good friends are better than riches in the bank, they say.'

'Well, I certainly enjoyed the day out with Tommy. It makes a change from working on the land. Things look different from out at sea . . . it all looks surprisingly clean and pretty. And Tommy was good company. He was telling me a story about a lad from Frizington fishing on Whitehaven pier.'

Bill then told the story Tommy had told him in the boat.

Jackson laughed as he listened to the tale, then sat back, his eyes twinkling merrily. 'A good story, lad. But did Tommy tell you about the time when him and his mate decided to imprison a lobster?'

'No. What happened?'

'Well, lad, they caught a lobster that was far too little to eat, so they decided to rock it up in a hole in a deep pool and feed it until it was fat. They found a deep pool just off the pier, put their lobster in it, and put a rock over the entrance so it wouldn't escape when the tide went out. They fed that lobster for weeks and weeks. Then, when it was big enough to eat, they decided to fetch it home. So the next morning they went down to the beach just as the tide was going out. But you'll never guess what had happened . . . It had gone! Somebody had watched them over the weeks and had decided, now that it was in its prime, to help themselves.'

'What a shame, Jackson, after all their work. There is so much wickedness in the world. . .' said Edith.

'There's just as much greed if you ask me. It serves them bloody well right for trying to steal a march on the others. You can't do that in Whitehaven – they're too bloody smart when it comes to getting owt for nowt!'

12

FOR SALE

'It looks like being a fine day today Esther – just the sort of Saturday when folk will be walking down to the beach. So you can get those bloody noisy pups, put them into the cart near the gateway and stick a ''For Sale'' notice on the side. We should sell them over the weekend if we're lucky.'

'Yes, Dad. They're a lovely mix of black and white, aren't they? How much should I charge for them?'

'Charge! Charge! I've never taken a penny for a pup in my life . . . Oh, but I forget, we're never had a bitch that you could remember anything about.'

'But you said I had to put a ''For Sale'' notice on the side of the cart.'

'Of course I did. If we put ''Pups Free'' near the public highway they'd all be gone before dinnertime – probably to folk who would only keep them for a week or so, just long enough to find out that first they eat, and then they piddle, usually on their best rug. But if they have to pay for them they'll think twice about coming in.'

'Won't Flash pine for them?'

'Not bloody likely. She's more fed up with them than I am. They give her no peace, wanting fed when she hasn't enough milk to feed them. Haven't you noticed that she keeps out of their way as much as she can? The next time she comes on heat I'll make sure she's locked in a hull for a few days – pups are more trouble than they're worth . . . Farming's about something more profitable and less trouble.'

'I haven't noticed Flash getting fed up with them. I've only watched the pups playing – no doubt they'll miss each other.'

'The little buggers are becoming a nuisance around the farm. They bark their heads off and that stupid Mollie goes straight to the barn to snuffle at the bottom of the door, in case they're not making enough din! That cow doesn't know whether she's a cow, a Herdwick or a wandering gypsy . . . And talking of wandering gypsies, Edith, did I hear you say that May was coming this morning?'

'Yes, I did. She's coming on the morning bus.'

'Well, I hope to God that Jim Lawson gets himself here before she does, then I'll be out of her way. He might take a fancy to some stirks and bullocks that I'm thinking of selling. A dealer like him could make me a decent offer – it would save trucking them to Whitehaven market. But he'll probably take his time getting up here from Ulverston. Farmers like to talk over a deal, so he could be an hour or two yet.'

Jackson stood and looked out of the window, watching his daughter bundling the puppies into the cart. Despite the excited yapping and youthful barking, she soon had them fairly well settled and the notice pinned to the side of the cart.

'A few new taties, a box of carrots and the odd turnip might tempt a few passers-by as well today, Edith . . . Get our Esther to make one or two more notices. She seems to manage the business side of things quite well. We should encourage her.'

'She gets more money at Sellafield than she can make at the farm gate, Jackson. But I'll ask her if she would like to keep an eye on a few things placed on the wall. Folk will have to make a meal when they get back home, so a few eggs and vegetables might save them going to the shop tomorrow.'

'Good God, Edith, you'd think we were a church fête. We're in this to make a living, not to be a convenience to folk that have nowt to do at home on a Saturday afternoon. Just look, a few of the early ones are coming this way. They must be the first to get off the bus.'

'Dear me, I must put the kettle on. Our May won't be far behind and she'll be dying for a cup of tea.'

'I reckon she will, but she won't be anywhere near the youngsters who've rushed off the bus first. She'll want to walk with someone in the same social class as herself. She won't have anything in common with folk who spend their free time on the beach.'

'She can be shy, Jackson. You shouldn't judge people by appearances.'

'*She* does. And there she is, walking behind that group of women pushing prams. They make more noise than them pups.'

Flash raised a surprised ear as the stranger opened the yard gate and stopped to speak to Esther, then stretched herself against the sunny wall to resume her peaceful doze, free from the responsibility of caring for her boisterous brood.

Jackson hastily picked up the nearest farming magazine and retreated to his armchair in the corner.

'I don't know what you've got so many pups for, Edith,' observed May as she came in. 'I counted seven, but they didn't stay still long enough for me to be sure how many there were. There could even be nine.'

'What's wrong with having a few pups, May?' demanded Jackson. 'We once had a bitch who had fourteen . . . She hadn't enough tits to go round.'

'Let me take your coat, May, and I'll hang it up on my way to make a cup of tea,' interrupted Edith swiftly, attempting to deflect this line of conversation.

But Jackson continued, pointing meaningfully to his magazine, *The Farmer and Stockbreeder* his finger underlining the last word of the title. 'Stockbreeders we are – we don't go in for any of these new-fangled birth pills I've been reading about in the papers. The only birth control medicine I'd use would be rat pills, to cut down them thieving buggers . . .'

'There's no need to be crude, nor to swear, Jackson,' his sister-in-law replied. 'Pups are a lot of work for Edith. They are difficult to house-train, especially when they come from a farm where they've been allowed to get into unhygienic ways.'

'I suppose if they're born in the middle of Egremont they come into the world with an automatic plumbing system?' the old farmer said sarcastically.

They're not usually allowed to dirty the inside of the house, Jackson. Townsfolk have no barns to put them in, so they have to train their pets from the start. A good thing too. We all have to learn self-control in order to live close together.'

'True enough, May,' agreed Edith. 'I'm sure you're ready for a cup of tea and a piece of cake after walking all the way from the bus stop. Jackson is only waiting for a dealer to come, then he'll be off round the stock. Anyway, it's nice to see you. Have you brought any news with you, or is everything quiet in Egremont?'

'You know me, Edith, I'm not one to gossip. Anything could be happening in Egremont and I wouldn't hear a word.'

Jackson's eyes peeped in disbelief over his magazine.

'But I wanted to let you know that I've booked to take a bus trip to Blackpool next Saturday.'

'I'm glad to hear that, May. It'll do you the world of good to get away,' smiled Edith as she passed her sister another piece of cake.

May nodded in agreement.

'Blackpool, May?' queried Jackson. 'I can't see you on the funfair somehow, but I suppose that folk you think you know well can always surprise you.'

'You don't think I'll be riding a funfair do you, Jackson?!' snapped May, her earrings glinting disdainfully. 'I've been persuaded by the vicar to join the rest of the Mothers' Union at the tea dance in the Tower Ballroom. I've brought my new silk dress for Edith to alter – it's a little tight across the bust.'

Jackson eyed his sister-in-law's ample bosom. 'Aye, you can't let your dress rip in the middle of your rhumba!'

May's eyes sparkled in annoyance as she faced Jackson over the table. 'Rhumba? Not on your life! An old-fashioned waltz and a foxtrot will do me nicely . . . If I want to make an exhibition of myself I only have to go to the Market Hall in Egremont on a Saturday night.'

'How do you know what goes on there on a Saturday night, May?' asked Jackson innocently.

'When I close the curtains before going to bed late on a Saturday night I've often seen couples making their way home . . . and the disgraceful things they get up to don't bear thinking about!'

'You could toss them a handful of them new birth control pills I've been hearing about lately. Pups are a bit easier to dispose of than what those folk are likely to get after a night out!'

'Take no notice of him, May,' interrupted Edith. 'I'm pleased that you're going with the Mothers' Union next week and I'll certainly have a look at your dress.'

'Tell me, May,' asked Jackson. 'At this tea dance, do you dance with men?'

'Of course we do! I might be lucky enough to meet a real gentleman and that would be very enjoyable.'

'The Market Hall wouldn't be the right place for you then. Only the locals go there and I shouldn't think there's a chap you could rightly call a gentleman in the town,' observed Jackson to himself.

'Cheerio Mam! Cheerio Aunt May! See you at teatime!' called Esther as she dashed down the stairs and hurriedly let herself out of the farmhouse.

'Where is *she* going?' asked Jackson. 'I thought she was selling eggs, taties and pups at the gate?'

'She's left an honesty box on the wall and a message to say that anyone who wants to buy a pup has to call at the house.'

'Where is she off to that's more important than selling at the door?'

'She's gone for a riding lesson. Didn't you notice her new trousers?'

'Riding lessons!' roared Jackson. 'What does she want riding lessons for? She stopped falling off our horses when she was about four years old! What need has she for fancy riding lessons?'

'Calm yourself, Jackson,' soothed May. 'The girl is right to learn the proper way. You know, there's two ways of doing most things – the rough way and the correct way. The only way I've seen her ride is bareback and no lady ever rides like that. She will learn to ride with the correct saddle and will learn poise and discipline. I certainly approve.'

'Who is going to pay for these lessons on poise and snobbery then?'

'She can pay for them herself, Jackson. She earns her own money now, so she can please herself,' said Edith boldly.

'And where can she stable and feed a riding horse if she has a notion to buy one? I can't afford to keep a useless animal that would probably upset Peggy and Captain . . . They're not used to flighty bits of horseflesh careering round the field and jumping over the fences. I only build my dykes high enough for heavy working horses. I don't have a corral to keep a steeple-chaser in.'

'Since she works at Sellafield now, Jackson, she'll be learning new ways of living that they know about in the south,' May lectured him. 'Knowing how to ride marks a girl out as different from the general run of girls. I'm pleased that a niece of mine is learning the ways of the gentry . . . in spite of uninformed opposition!'

'I reckon she'll have to go to the south to find a chap who's able to keep her. Such extravagance is far beyond my means, and . . .' he looked suspiciously in his wife's direction, 'I don't think you've been asking her for enough money for her keep, if she can entertain such high-class notions.'

The sound of a car entering the farmyard brought the conversation to a welcome end, at least from Edith's point of view.

Jim Lawson came into the kitchen, and was pleased to be introduced to May.

'What a courteous man!' she exclaimed, when he and Jackson had left to view the cattle.

'Yes, he has a pleasant way with him,' agreed Edith. 'I suppose he has to charm the farmers and their wives in order to make a few bargains. His way of life wouldn't suit me, though. He's always on the move and nothing ever belongs to him for any length of time. Anyway, let's have a look at your dress.'

* * *

'A smart-looking woman, your sister-in-law, Jackson. I'm surprised she's still a widow.'

'If you judge a beast as badly as you judge women, Jim, I'll have no trouble getting rid of these good-looking bullocks.'

Jim laughed. 'I couldn't keep my wife. She left me for a chap who worked regular hours. I think she has a grown-up family now. But if I could meet a classy woman past the first flush of youth she might settle all right with me. Ulverston is a nice place to live.'

'I don't think May would be the right one for you, Jim . . . In fact I can't think of anyone off hand who I would wish her on. Besides, Ulverston isn't far enough south for her. She has highfalutin' notions about the proper way to live. Ulverston might appeal to her for a short while, but she'd soon realise that it's cut off from civilisation . . . I mean, its only claim to fame is its cattle market . . . oh, and that famous comedian who lived there.'

'Stan Laurel.'

'Aye, well, May isn't keen on either comedy or cows. Why don't you settle for the good life you have, instead of wishing calamity on yourself? Are you going to take them bullocks or not? I've named my price.'

Jim chuckled. 'I'll take them, Jackson. You know, there's nothing like a few words with you to sort a chap out! I was going to invite myself for tea, but seeing as you think the lady's beyond me I'll just settle for the bullocks. The lorry will call next Monday afternoon.'

* * *

'You're generous with your money tonight, John,' observed Tom Graham, reaching for his drink at the bar of the Grey Mare that evening.

'I should think most of us can afford to be generous

tonight. Jim Lawson seems to have visited every farm in the neighbourhood and he told me he'd bought the best stock he's seen this year. You're looking pleased with yourself, Jackson. No doubt you sold him them bullocks you've been feeding up for the last few months.'

Jackson looked up from his game of dominoes. 'Aye, I did very well today, John. It wasn't just the bullocks though.'

He paused to lay a domino, knowing that his listeners would be waiting for him to elaborate.

'This morning I had a few things for sale. Seven pups and plenty of stuff for the women to buy on their way back from the shore. By the end of the day, I'd sold all my bullocks, seven pups, all my foodstuff and had a good offer for Edith's sister. A chap couldn't ask for better luck than that.'

'Why did you turn down the offer for May? She's always struck me as a fine-looking woman,' observed John seriously.

'If it had been you making the offer I might have considered it, but it was a nice chap who doesn't deserve a worse hand than life has already dealt him!'

'How about dealing your next hand now?' laughed John Steel. 'Or are you afraid that *your* luck has run out?'

13

A Tale of the Riverbank

The sound of Peggy's hooves echoed and re-echoed between the high walls on either side of the rough road, as Jackson, standing in the middle of the empty cart, drove the mare home past the village of Low Mill. The occupants of the houses came to their doors to greet whichever local farmer was passing through.

Jackson called out to everyone by name, while the eager mare continued homewards. His eye was caught by the war memorial, as it always was. He knew every name on it, including the VC – a VC from a small place like this!

There had been no war memorials in his youth. *Then* the two world wars were tragedies still to come. He slowed down to scan the list of familiar names. Why a memorial? Who here would forget them? Was it so that future generations would learn to live in peace? Was that the reason they had been built the length and breadth of the country? He shook the reins gently and Peggy accelerated.

A tune that Edith often sang floated through Jackson's mind: 'Look at the tombstone, marble with nobs on;/ Wouldn't it be nice to be blooming well dead!'

He shook his head slightly, then waved to the folk who greeted him from the row of cottages facing the river.

Soon they reached the bridge. Jackson glanced over – he could see the water running swift and high, coloured red by the iron ore which had leached from the pit banks upstream. The red dye had begun its race for the sea during a rainstorm, then washed down the small streams to join the main watercourse, giving the Ehen its nickname 'the red river'.

Jackson spied a long stiff fishing rod, which suddenly bent double, then straightened again. As he crossed the bridge, he was just in time to see a plump fish thrown, flapping, on to the riverbank.

Peggy reluctantly slowed down, anticipating the 'Hello Jackson!' that she usually heard when she crossed the bridge. Sure enough, a gruff voice rose from the depths beneath the road. Peggy instantly prepared to sample the tasty grass that grew along the hedge beside the bridge.

Jackson tied the reins to the side of the cart and lowered himself down to join his friend who was fishing at the edge of the beck.

Jackson didn't know a lot about fishing but he had watched this river over a lifetime and knew its changing moods. One day it could be a gentle, trickling stream; the next, an angry torrent, racing past farms and houses, ignoring bridges, and even rolling cobbles and boulders noisily along the river bed in its haste to reach the sea.

Fish, eager to reach their spawning grounds, have the good sense to sneak upstream through the quieter eddies at the edge of the swirling river. They sense that they are safe, hidden beneath the ore-coloured water. Local fishermen knew their habits well. The paths down to the beck were always well trodden when the river enjoyed a flood. Like all towns built on a river crossing, Egremont and its river have been entwined together for generations, each owing the other so much. No wonder the Egremont coat of arms sports three fishes.

'Have you caught many, Moses? That's a fine-looking one you've just landed.' Jackson glanced admiringly at the fish beside him. Its scales were so bright, he guessed it must have been swimming in the sea just hours earlier.

'Aye, one or two sea trout. The run is fairly good today.'

'Fairly good,' laughed Jackson. 'I've never yet heard you, or any fisherman, say that the fishing was good. There's always something wrong. I reckon the truth is that the little buggers are too clever for you. It stands to reason, if you need all that tackle to catch a small fish they must be gay crafty la'al things.'

Moses laughed. Such a remark was no more than he expected from his friend.

'How do you know exactly where to fish?

'You look at the height of the water on the pillars on the bridge. We each have our own marker – a certain stone. That's how I know the depth of the water below the beck edges and where the gravel banks are beneath the surface. Fish don't like to feel mud under them. The spate·water stirs it up and clogs their gills.'

'Well, I didn't know there was owt like that to consider.'

'Oh, there's a darn sight more . . . And, as I keep telling our Sally when she complains about the time I spend down by the river, you can't catch fish in the dolly tub!'

Moses put another small worm on to his fish hook, waited for the line to straighten, then lowered it upstream at the very edge of the river.

In no time he struck another fish which he flicked expertly on to the riverbank. It flapped its annoyance in a spray of water, before Moses despatched it. The two fish now lay gleaming side by side on the fresh grass, their silvery skins mottled with round black sea lice.

'Fourteen inches – both of them,' said Moses approvingly, running his hand lightly down the slippery scales.

Jackson had by now settled himself near the fisherman. 'You must be fishing "stuff", Moses, to catch them so fast.'

'Not me,' he replied indignantly. 'I know the rules and I stick to them. You'll never find *me* fishing salmon roe . . . It's illegal, whatever you choose to call it. I only use worms – there's nothing better for fishing under the edge during a flood.'

'Well you must be bloody good at it then, Moses.'

He watched, as Moses baited, then lowered the cumbersome, ancient-looking rod over the edge of the near bank into the fast-flowing river. Both men were standing well back from the river's edge to avoid disturbing any fish which might be feeding under it.

Jackson watched his friend handling the long one-piece

rod and marvelled, as he always did, at the patience of the local fishermen, who had to walk to the River Ehen – because their rods were too long to fit inside a bus! In the house they were kept propped up in the staircase, as there was rarely a room high enough or long enough to house them.

'I don't remember ever seeing you having a go at the fishing game, Jackson . . . I've often wondered why. I know you like a bit of snaring and shooting, so why not fishing?'

'Well, the reason is simple. Our Edith's niece is married to Ned Smith – one of the best poachers in the district – so I've never seen why I should learn to do something that takes so long to master, especially when we have an expert in the family. You know, Moses, we rarely buy a bit of fish. If our Edith went into that fish shop in Egremont they wouldn't have a notion who she was.'

'Yes, I forgot that Ned was related to Edith somehow.'

'Yes, our Edith's family don't usually marry anybody I approve of – they all fancy themselves a bit – so I reckon Lily is about the best of lot. Our Edith has her doubts about Ned, but we never tell her how he comes by the fish . . . After all, it's a bit daft upsetting folk about something they don't understand.'

'She'll understand well enough if he ever gets caught.'

'Not much chance of that happening now. No doubt you'll remember that Ned's father was the gamekeeper and beck-watcher for his lordship?'

'I know that well enough, one of the best they ever had up at the Hall.'

'True, true. His father taught him all he knew, thinking that he would take over from him when he retired . . . But Ned realised that he could do much better for himself if he found a job and did his bit of poaching after work. No, Moses. I knew Lily wouldn't ever have an empty pot if she married Ned.'

'I should think you won't have an empty pot either, eh Jackson?!'

'Isn't that what relatives are for? A gamekeeper turned poacher is a bit like a policeman turned criminal – they know all the tricks of the trade. Ned's father has tried hard enough to catch him, but, like any good father, he's taught him too much, too well.'

Jackson stood up when he heard Peggy take another step. 'Stand still!' he shouted in her direction.

The mare raised her head obediently, her mouth full of fresh juicy grass. She kept her head up as long as she could, munching slowly, to show her master that she had ceased both to graze and to wander onwards in the direction of their farm.

The minute Jackson's conversation resumed, she lowered her head to nibble the tasty grass, but was more careful about moving forward in case the rattling cart betrayed her.

She had once been walking along the road grazing innocently, only to discover that the shaft had buried itself in the hedge and the wheel had mounted up the side, fixing her in an uncomfortable position. It had taken a lot of cursing by her master and much uncomfortable backing and pushing for her before the cart had returned to its correct position on the road. She didn't want all that fuss again. Surely her master could trust her to graze without making the same mistake again. After all, she was much older and more experienced now. But humans often didn't understand that horses could learn things quite fast. She shook her head in exasperation and her bridle rattled.

'You can just do as you're told,' snarled Jackson in her direction. He turned back to his friend. 'That bloody mare doesn't like being told to behave herself. Did you hear that bridle shaking? And just look at them ears stuck back . . . You'd think she'd read her own pedigree.'

'She looks like a decent mare to me; there aren't many would graze away like that while their owner sat and talked a fair distance from the road. John Steel hardly has time to say a word when he crosses this bridge – his horses move off as soon as his feet touch the ground.'

'He's different, Moses. He doesn't keep control of his animals. They know he's always in a big rush to get somewhere or other, so the horses are always dashing about as well. Now me, I've always taken my time about things. Life has to be lived at a slow pace – you fishermen know all about that. If you fuss, you frighten the fish away.'

'That's true enought, Jackson. They say that everything comes to them that sit and wait.'

'There you are then. Them poor horses that work for John Steel daren't stop in case they feel his temper across their backs. The silly bugger has too many mares in foal at the same time, so he comes to borrow Peggy every now and again, and she needs a week's rest afterwards!'

Peggy's head was lifted and her ears pricked uneasily. She had heard her name mentioned at least twice and she wasn't sure whether she was in some sort of trouble. Anyway, she'd better keep her head up, just in case her master was watching her.

The voices continued – at a lower pitch. 'Good,' thought Peggy 'I'm all right for another few bites.' She lowered her head and gingerly edged herself forward, taking care not to let the huge wheels clunk as she moved along.

'Yes, Jackson,' continued Moses. 'You're very lucky to have someone like Ned in the family. Not like me – a few fish just provide one or two extra meals now and again. And besides, it's more of a hobby than anything else.'

'I bet it costs quite a bit by the time you've paid for the licence and the permit.'

'Aye, it does, and the tackle is a pricey item as well.'

'What about the bait – is that costly?'

'The best bait is worms, and finding good worms is a bit of a problem – our garden hasn't had a decent worm in it for a year or two now. They say that worms are good for the soil, so that's probably why my leeks are no thicker than your walking stick.'

'Now that's a fact, Moses. I like to see plenty of worms in my fields – you can always tell which farm has a decent crop of worms in the spring by the flocks of seagulls that follow the plough. If you see me ploughing in one field and John Steel ploughing next door you'll notice that they all jostle about to get a good dive down to my land.'

'Why's that then? Surely the next field will have as many worms in it as yours?'

'I'd expect a miner to think like that – you don't know any better I suppose.'

'What do you mean?'

'Well, even you must admit that worms would hardly climb over a dyke – or burrow underneath – they're not rabbits!'

'I know that, but surely the two fields are the same?'

'No, lad! Nothing could be further from the truth. The fields can be next to each other but if the farming is different then the two fields are different.'

'Can worms be farmed differently?'

'Certainly they can. The secret of good worm farming, and consequently good arable farming, is the sort of muck you put on the land. Fat healthy worms are the result of good feeding and good breeding during the winter. Decent hull muck is a priceless item for the farmer . . . Next time you walk down to the river, just kick a bit of newly scaled muck with your boot and see how much is pure muck and how much is straw mixed in. Look for worms that have travelled through the stirks, if there are any. Then take a good sniff. If you *have* to have a good sniff then you needn't stop to dig for worms – the best muck meets you before you know which field it's in. You can walk past some fields and never know that owt had been spread on them. That means the stock have spent a hungry winter inside, licking walls and chewing hull doors and suchlike.

Then they've been turned out like walking hat racks in the spring.'

'I've never noticed things like that, Jackson.'

'Well, it's no wonder you have a job knowing where to dig for worms. Now I'll tell you what. Any time you care to get your bike out, have a ride to that big field just past our house and dig in that as much as you like. The best bit is up by the dyke nearest the farm – you won't find better worms in the district.'

'That's grand, Jackson, I'll certainly take a trip out there when I run short of a few worms.'

The waiting rod shook as they spoke.

'Here we go, I reckon I've got a good catch. Hang on a minute, Jackson, and give me a hand to land this – it feels like a strong 'un.'

Jackson watched as his friend played then landed another big sea trout.

'You can take this one home, Jackson. I've had a good catch today – it'll be a change for you from tatie pot and pasties.'

'Tatie pot be damned. There's a brace of pheasant hanging up in our back kitchen, fresh from his lordship's land.'

'You've been shooting again then, Jackson?'

'No, our Esther has been complaining about too much shot in her dinner – lasses are never satisfied these days you know – so Ned fetched a couple of young birds without a blemish on them.'

'Oh come on! Don't try to tell me they gave themselves up?!'

'Like I said before, Moses, you've got to know the tricks of the trade. Lily only had to sprinkle a few handfuls of sultanas that had been soaked in meths, and they keeled over very nicely after their dinner. I didn't even have to waste the price of a cartridge on them.'

Moses laughed as he re-baited his line. 'All I can say is that I'm pleased I'm not fishing the Irt like Ned does. I'd be lucky if there was anything left to catch . . . Not that we're short of poachers on this beck – but they don't seem to be as successful as Ned.'

'Successful he certainly is. You know, I was down at his house the other day and he had just come in and emptied his pockets on to the table. Several pounds he had – and you'll never guess who had paid him good money for a bagful of salmon.'

'Who?'

'The squire's housekeeper! "What lovely fresh salmon . . ." Jackson mimicked the shrill tones of Mrs James at the big house. "And just at the right time. We've guests coming this weekend." '

Jackson roared with laughter as he related the tale. 'The silly woman didn't realise that the salmon was only fresh because Ned had just clicked it out of the beck on the squire's land, a few yards out of sight of his drawing-room window!'

'So the squire paid for his own fish?'

'Yes, and it serves him right for employing somebody who can't spot a poacher.'

'Well, I prefer to enjoy my fishing, Jackson, even if it means paying for it. I've seen some lovely sights here on my own by the beck . . . especially at night time. Only a few months ago I was sitting very quietly down below the bridge (it was a still evening) when suddenly something caught my eye at the other side of the beck. I sat quietly and watched. Sure enough, I saw a dark tail move quickly, so I knew it was a stoat – awful shy things, as you know.'

Jackson nodded as he reached in his pocket for a piece of chewing tobacco and his penknife.

'Well, it looked around and sniffed the air, not noticing me. Then, would you believe it – it started to dance on its hind legs! It pranced around in circles thoroughly enjoying itself. It had a pause, and off it went again – circling, jumping, twirling – and finally finished off with a couple of somersaults. Then it disappeared. I asked a few folk if they

had seen anything like that and I was told that in the
mating season the young males like to practise their
courtship dance where nobody can watch them, so I was
very privileged. But I don't expect a farmer like you to
believe me; most folk reckoned I'd been on the bottle.'

'No such thing, Moses. The folk I know who've been on
the bottle and have hallucinations seem to see things like
pink elephants, and I don't reckon they'd recognise a stoat
if they saw one. Besides, hares do the same thing. That's
why they're called "mad March hares", so I'm sure you
can have "mad March stoats". Just don't tell the tale in the
Grey Mare . . . They never believe anything they haven't
seen with their own eyes.'

Moses laughed and continued. 'No, I like to be on the
right side of the law. I remember old Jack from up
Frizington way. He poached for years, and was caught one
night as he was making his way back from the Ehen beck.

He was stopped by a policeman. "Been down the beck then, Jack?" the policeman asked. "Yes, but I didn't go fishing." "Empty your pockets," the policeman ordered. And sure enough, he found a fish hidden away in his poacher's pocket, inside the lining of his coat . . . No, I wouldn't like to take a risk like that.'

'Aye, but maybe you didn't hear about the next time Jack went down the river and the policeman stopped him again and he put his hand in the poacher's pocket and a big vicious ferret just about bit two of the policeman's fingers off!'

'Go on!'

'I bet he didn't put his hand in a bag or a pocket in a big rush after that. They reckoned he had his hand bandaged for a good three weeks. Fingers are bad to heal if they've been bitten by an animal that's used to catching rats and suchlike . . . No, Moses, I wouldn't like to tangle with a professional poacher.'

'You're right. I wouldn't like to cross one myself and I'm a keen fisherman. It's a good thing to know where to be on a dark night when the fish are biting.'

'And the job can be a bit complicated. I remember Ned had promised to catch a big salmon for a chap who asked him to deliver it to Eskdale Show. Ned agreed and went off to catch the salmon. The one he caught was a fine sixteen pounder – just the job for the chap who wanted it. But Ned then had the task of carrying it into the show field without being spotted – although he managed.'

'How?' asked an interested Moses.

'He thought hard, then got the idea of tying it round his waist!'

'I wouldn't have thought of that,' laughed Moses.

'That's why you've got to be a thinker if you want to outwit the law. Ned manages fine.'

Jackson looked in the direction of his horse and cart. 'Good God! Look where that mare has wandered to! If I don't get going she'll be home before me. I should have stopped to talk on the outward journey when she was pulling a heavy load, with her nose pointing away from home. She wouldn't have gone gallivanting off like this . . . Remember to dig a few worms next time you're down our way!' he called over his shoulder as he hurried to catch up with Peggy.

* * *

A week or so later, Jackson was sitting down for his supper. 'You're late tonight, Jackson,' said Edith.

'I stayed to finish cutting that far hay field; I didn't see the sense in leaving half an acre or so for tomorrow morning – and it's light until late these days.'

'I told the sergeant you might be late and it would be better to come back tomorrow.'

Jackson looked up sharply from his dinner. 'What on earth was the police sergeant doing here? I've been too busy lately to break any of his laws.'

'*You* haven't done anything, Jackson. Apparently some of the farmers near Egremont have been complaining about folk coming out of the town and pinching potatoes and vegetables from the fields . . .'

'That doesn't happen here – we're too far away. If anybody wants to steal a few poor-looking taties near Egremont, they're welcome to them. As usual, he's making a half-hour job last all day.'

'That's where you're wrong, Jackson . . . He found a man digging in that big tatie field on the corner. He intended to steal, or so the policeman said, because he had a bag and a big tin on his bike.'

Jackson lowered his knife and fork in amazement. 'Who in Egremont would bother to come all this way just for our taties when they could steal Tom's best a good mile nearer?'

'The chap said he knew you and that you'd given him permission to dig as much as he liked in your field . . . for worms. An unlikely story I think, and the sergeant thought so too . . . As he said, you can dig for worms anywhere in Egremont itself. But the chap said that you had fatter and better worms than anybody else. That's why he had come this far. However the sergeant was kind and just gave him a caution, seeing as you weren't here to deal with it yourself.'

'Did the fella give his name?'

'Moses somebody or other – I forget his last name.'

Jackson's face cleared as all was revealed. 'Moses! Moses Kenmare! Yes, I know him . . . He's better off when he stays by the river in the bulrushes!' he chuckled to his perplexed wife.

14

MUCK-SPREADING

'What on earth's the big rush for this morning, Dad?' asked a flustered Bill. 'I've finished the milking at least an hour earlier than usual. The cows are almost having nervous breakdowns ... Mollie looked at me as if I'd committed murder when Flash hustled them through the field gate. She was too early to see the school bus go by, and you know how she like to dawdle in front of a noisy vehicle. She'll just have to make do with looking over the gate this morning.'

'I want some muck spread on that big ten acre – early!' snapped his father. 'I've caught Peggy and she's ready saddled, so you'd better have your breakfast and get loaded up.'

'I bet Peggy got a shock when you fetched her in before breakfast . . .'

'What do you take me for? Since when do I have to ask the bloody horse if she's ready to get up!'

Bill knew it was futile to argue when his father was in this mood.

'Look at the rain pouring down, Mother,' he complained. 'That field will have so much water in the bottom corner that passing shelducks are likely to settle on it. Last year they did, and he was boasting in the pub that our wildlife surpassed that of the Solway estuary . . . Where he found out about what lives on the Solway beats me!'

'It's that subscription for *National Geographic* that Jane bought him last Christmas. He reads those magazines all the time . . . Your father has a very enquiring mind.'

'Some of it might be "enquiring", but most of it is just "cussed"!'

'Try telling him that yourself,' laughed Esther. 'You'd

better hurry. He's coming across the yard as fast as he did when he ate too much goose last Christmas!'

'That's enough, Esther,' warned her mother. 'You know how much your father enjoys a fat goose.'

'But even you must admit that he never usually leads muck on a soggy wet day.'

'Still sitting here then?' snapped Jackson as he sat down to his bacon, eggs and black pudding. 'Once you get loaded up and away, I'll set off to follow you. Then I'll start scaling it . . . We'll soon finish a little field like that.'

'But it's raining, Dad,' observed Esther.

Jackson glanced up sharply. 'Unlike you, Esther, *I've* actually set foot outside this morning. I know exactly what sort of weather it is.'

The farmhouse kitchen suddenly cleared of all but Jackson and an uneasy Flash.

* * *

It was cold as well as wet when Bill started to load the cart. The level of the muck had risen over the months under the stirks. They had trampled it under their feet, making it heavy work to fork out. Soon the sweat was trickling down Bill's neck and collecting under his collar. A fine hazy sheen of rain covered Peggy's back and harness as she stood outside the hull, with the cart backed up against the open door.

'I'll make this load as big and heavy as I can,' thought Bill. 'Peggy's fresh, and I'll be finished sooner.'

Another quarter of an hour and they were off . . . Peggy shook her bridle, sending a fine spray across Bill's back as he turned to climb up, holding a potato bag to sit on in front of the uninviting load.

'You needn't bloody well blame me for this,' he snapped in the direction of the two flattened ears.

The only good thing about it was that Jackson had let him have Peggy who could be relied upon to walk

161

obediently up and down while he forked the muck out of the back of the cart into small heaps, ready for his father to spread over the field.

Bill sat behind Peggy's dripping rump and watched her feet splashing through the puddles on the narrow road. The load behind him smelt ripe. It was a good smell on a crisp frosty day . . . But on a day like this, it was just a dripping brown heap, getting heavier and heavier by the minute. He glanced behind him and saw a tobacco-coloured trail following them down the middle of the country road.

Another good thing was that the huge iron-clad wheels, which had graced their carts until only a week or so ago, had been replaced by new, modern rubber-tyred ones. The almost silent swish of the tyres behind him promised an easier day's work.

They had reached the gate. Bill jumped stiffly down from his perch and opened it, his feet sinking in the mud which had been churned up by the stock.

'Come on, Peg. Let's get on with the job.' Peggy sank her shoulders obediently into her collar and heaved the cart, but soon stopped as the wheels quickly buried themselves in the deep mud . . . She tried again but the wheels reached new, unaccustomed depths.

'Good God,' cursed Bill. 'This *would* have to happen, especially on a morning like this!' And just to compound his misery he could see his father approaching, riding a bicycle, his fork balanced over his shoulder.

He urged Peggy to have one more try . . . but it was no use. The small wheels had sunk in as far as their hubs.

'What the hell are you doing?' asked Jackson as he swung down from his bicycle seat.

He took in the scene – Peggy waiting patiently for a sensible command, the shafts tipped as high as her belly band allowed, the tailboard of the cart only just clearing the swimming mud (mud which was rapidly changing colour to a richer and deeper brown).

'Well, don't just stand there! Pull some thorns out of the dyke to put under them wheels whle I fork some of this stuff off. I see you were daft enough to overload the bloody thing. You'd need a team of forestry horses to pull it out of this sludge!'

*   *   *

Edith and Esther were busy preparing a hot midday meal for father and son as soon as they returned from the field.

'I can't understand what got into Dad this morning, there was no looking at him!'

'Yes, he was restless all night, then got up an hour early . . . I could hear him telling Bill that it was time he was out of bed. Something must be bothering him, but we'll find out about it in good time. He's not the worrying sort. It's me who does the worrying for the two of us!'

163

A rattle from the farm gate made Esther look up. 'Here's Tom Graham, Mam. I wonder what's brought him this way on such a nasty day.'

Tom was soon in the kitchen, warming his hands at the fire. 'There's a good smell coming from your oven, Edith.'

'I'm cooking a steak and kidney pie for Jackson and Bill. They'll be wet and hungry when they get home . . . But what brings you here on such a nasty day?'

'I called because it *is* nasty. I thought Jackson would be inside and would have five minutes for a crack.'

'Oh, is that all?' asked a relieved Edith.

'What on earth has he decided to do on a wet day like this?'

'Muck-spreading . . . They were both up early this morning and off – rain or no rain.'

Tom laughed heartily. 'Well, I'll be damned . . . he's decided he's going to win the bet then?'

'What bet?'

Tom glanced uneasily at Edith's thunderstruck expression.

'Am I speaking out of turn? Did he not tell you about the bet they made last night?'

'No, you're not speaking out of turn, Tom. Have this mug of tea Esther's made for you and we'll all sit down and hear about it.'

A sheepish Tom realised that honesty was his best policy.

'We were talking about how useful a tractor is. John Steel reckoned that Jackson should have bought one last year when he had that demonstration. He maintained that tractors could beat a horse hands down on the heavy farm work.'

Edith nodded with an understanding air.

'They had both had little too much to drink if you ask me . . .'

'That's Dad,' agreed Esther.

'Well, things heated up a bit, and Jackson told Alan to put his tractor where his mouth was . . .'

'I've always said that when the drink's in – the sense is out,' Edith remarked drily.

'That's as may be, Edith, but it ended up with Jackson challenging Alan to a sort of competition.'

'A competition?' Esther was amused at the thought.

'I might have guessed by his mood this morning that he'd got himself into a fix that he couldn't get out of!' snapped Edith. 'Tell me, what was he stupid enough to bet?'

'He bet that he could spread more acres with muck over the next two days with a horse and cart than Alan could with a tractor and trailer. We told them that the weather forecast was heavy rain, and it would be very soft on the land, but neither of them were put off in the slightest.'

'And if he loses the bet?'

'He pays for a round of drinks . . . and last night the pub was full! A chap from Egremont said they were setting up a betting board. One of them hound trailing chaps – they'll have a bet on owt.'

'What are the odds on Dad winning?' asked Esther, intrigued.

'It's a disgrace,' snapped her mother. 'No wonder he said nothing about it this morning – making a fool of himself in the pub. And there were bound to be some sensible people listening to such rubbish.'

'It'll get all round Egremont . . . If Aunt May hears she'll emigrate or something,' chuckled Esther.

'I happened to notice Alan Steel loading up *his* trailer when I drove past his yard. Muck and water were splashing all over the spot!'

'It's amazing what two normally sensible men will do after a drop of drink and a bit of provocation – from so-called *friends*.'

Tom was pleased that he'd finished his drink and

biscuits . . . He was only too keen to get away before Jackson got back.

Half an hour later, two wet and stinking members of the family arrived home.

Their dinner was placed on the table in the scullery.

'I'm not having you two trailing that muck into the kitchen,' said Edith, 'especially when there was no need to lead muck on a day like today.'

'I believe in getting on with any job that's sitting looking at me, Mother. A drop of rain doesn't bother me.'

'But a drop of ale has an instant effect on you, or so I hear . . .'

Jackson looked up in alarm, as Bill glanced questioningly at a giggling Esther.

'Who's been here, telling tales, this morning?'

'A good neighbour.'

'A bloody nosey parker . . . Had he called on Alan Steel to see if *he'd* started work this morning as well?'

'Oh yes. Two daft men have soaked themselves to the skin for no good reason. And the smell is worse than usual . . .'

'What am I missing then?' asked a puzzled Bill.

'Dad bet Alan Steel a round of drinks that he could spread more muck in two days with a horse and cart than Alan could with his tractor and trailer!' explained Esther delightedly.

'Great! Hurry up, Dad. You're wasting time . . . If we're going to win the bet we'll have to move faster than this.'

'Make sure you don't fill the cart too full this time, lad. A few more lighter loads will do the trick, then we won't get bogged down again,' Jackson explained as they made their way through the back door.

'Leave that door open for a bit, Esther,' called Edith. 'Rain or no rain, we'll have to let a bit of fresh air into this kitchen.'

'I wish women could go into pubs. I'd love to hear the crack next Sunday!'

*   *   *

The Grey Mare was full as usual the next Sunday night.

'I wonder if Harry Jepson walked the fields and judged the competition last Wednesday?' Tom Graham asked the bar in general.

'All I know is that my van has been caked in stinking cow muck from the roads for the last five days,' said Joe Watson. 'Some of my customers asked if the cold meat had gone off . . . Them two warring farmers have cost me hard cash this week.'

'You should have borrowed my pony and trap,' offered another drinker. 'Muck doesn't stick so much to thin wheels and a pony's feet.'

'I've enough to do to keep control of a vehicle that I can switch on and off, and stands still if I leave it, without tackling something that's got a mind of its own!'

'So you've bet on Alan?'

'That's right.'

Jackson entered the bar, and beamed at the waiting crowd. 'What are you all looking at? The judge hasn't arrived yet . . . You all seem to have money burning a hole in your pockets!'

They laughed companionably, as more people made their way to their favourite seats. Jean was pleased . . . The bet, stupid as it was, had brought a lot of customers to the pub, even though it was yet another wet night.

Alan Steel, who was full of cold and had lost his voice, had taken his usual place.

Soon everybody was assembled. Harry Jepson brought the gathering to order when they all had drinks in their hands. 'Glad to see you, Alan. I know you've been in bad fettle these last few days.'

'If he's daft enough to ride round on a tractor all day in the pouring rain, he deserves all he gets,' observed Jean from the bar.

'That's right,' nodded Jackson.

167

'Anyhow,' continued Harry, glancing at a small note-book he had drawn from his pocket, 'I walked the fields as you all asked me . . . Both farmers had managed to spread muck over twenty acres which is a good two days' work.'

'What about the thickness?' asked the Egremont bookie, quickly making calculations. 'There must be some way of judging this competition.'

Harry held his hand up for silence. 'The thickness was exactly the same. Both farmers know what they're doing . . .' He felt the impatience of the listening crowd. 'So I had to make a closer examination of the fields to see what they looked like when the work was finished.'

He flicked the page over as he spoke.

'Come on then. What did you decide?' asked the eager bookie.

Harry slowly perused his notes, enjoying his moment of glory, then leant back in his chair with an air of finality. 'So I knew I had to make a decision on the smartness of the field . . . Jackson had closed the gates, but the deep ruts and mud in the gateway told me that he'd had a right struggle getting the horse and cart in and out a few times.'

Jackson lowered his drink, his hand feeling in his pocket for his money.

'Then I went back to Alan's fields and had another close look at them. Both gates were left open. He must have been too tired to get off the tractor and close them.'

Jackson's face brightened.

'I also saw that he'd churned the fields up an awful lot – like a World War One battlefield it was. In fact he'd had to dig the heavy trailer out in a few places . . . So I must declare Jackson the winner – by a long wet day!'

The two farmers shook hands, as Jean started taking orders at the bar, while the bookie honoured his bets at a corner table.

'Let's have another competition, Jackson, on a good frosty morning,' whispered Alan as he accompanied his opponent to the bar.

'I don't reckon Edith would allow that. We've been nearer to a divorce this last week than we've ever been,' chuckled Jackson, reaching for his tot of rum.

15

CONISTON

Jackson entered the farm kitchen and sat down to breakfast.

His heart sank as he noticed Edith reading a letter which must have arrived while he was out milking. Letters always came from his wife's family. Jackson's relatives weren't in the habit of writing.

What did it mean? Edith didn't seem agitated so there couldn't have been a death. She seemed very pleased . . . Whatever she was reading must herald some sort of disturbance to the pleasant rhythm of his life. Jackson was very suspicious.

'A letter this morning then?' he ventured, reaching for his knife and fork.

Edith looked up. 'Ah, you've come in . . . Just help yourself to a bit of breakfast. I'm reading this letter from our Sally.'

Edith's cousin Sally lived in a remote row of miners' cottages near Coniston. She wrote once or twice a year, and occasionally Edith went to visit her.

Jackson watched his wife's animated expression as she read the letter. 'Sally has invited us to spend a few days with them,' she said.

'Is one of them ill?' asked a dismayed Jackson.

'No, why?'

'Well, if no one's ill, there really isn't any reason to go all that way. I mean, if someone was dying it would be different . . . you'd *have* to go.'

Esther came in as he spoke. 'Who wants us to go where, Mam?'

'Your mother has been invited to go gallivanting off to Coniston when no one's ill. Can you understand that?'

'I can't see that anybody's got to be ill before we go to visit our relatives in Coniston,' argued Esther.

'Yes,' agreed her mother, 'we could both go. After all, there isn't a lot on hand here.'

'Not a lot on hand!' fumed Jackson. 'Only the ploughing and harrowing . . . And our Jane's not here this spring. I can't see us managing.'

'I love the train journey,' continued Esther, ignoring her father.

'So do I, especially the run from Foxfield to Coniston. It's like riding through a wonderland, what with all the hills so close . . .'

'And the names of the stations . . . Broughton, Woodland and Torver. They're quite different from the coastal line,' added Esther.

Jackson was very alarmed at this turn in the conversation. 'If you fancy a ride on a railway what's wrong with having a day out on the Ratty? The scenery is the best in the north of England! What's more, you'd be back for suppertime. Or even a day trip to Silloth – it's ages since you've been to Silloth . . .'

'I love the Ratty, Dad – it's a great ride on a warm summer's day – but spending a few days in Coniston will be a real treat . . . And it'll be lovely to see Sally and the family.'

Jackson's heart sank. He had a feeling he was losing this battle.

'And if we have time we might take the bus to Ambleside and see how our Lizzie and her kids are getting on,' suggested Edith.

What a pity I didn't check how far away Edith's family had chosen to settle before I married her, thought Jackson to himself.

The two women had got the bit well and truly between their teeth now.

'That would be great, Mam. I haven't seen them for

171

ages, and Ambleside is such a lovely place to spend a day or two . . .'

A day or two! It was beginning to sound as though the pair of them were planning to spend all spring wandering about among their relatives' houses, like visiting royalty, thought a disgruntled Jackson.

'The bit I enjoy is going to Sally's lavatory,' enthused Esther.

This remark was too much for Jackson. 'Lavatory? You mean to tell me you plan to go all the way to Coniston to sit on somebody else's closet! What's wrong with the one we've got at home? I managed to get a new-fangled water closet fixed *inside* the bloody house for you . . . but likely that's not good enough. You have to travel all the way to Lancashire to find something better. What have they got up in the miners' cottages that's so special then?'

'I forget that you've never been to Sally's house, Dad. You won't know that they haven't even got electricity yet and they certainly don't need a water lavatory . . .'

'Well, what have they got that's so much better than all the modern conveniences I've bought you in recent years?'

Esther continued her description excitedly. 'Their lavatory isn't in, or even very near the house. You have to walk the length of the row of houses, then you see a small row of toilets. But they're built *over* the beck that runs from the top of the mountain behind the houses, then runs *under* the seats of the lavatory and continues down the mountainside to join the big river at the bottom . . . And, in addition, the seat has *two* holes in it, so two people can go to the lavatory together!'

Jackson's face registered disbelief. 'To think that a daughter of mine would be prepared to travel by rail – and have to wait I don't know how long on Foxfield station to catch a branch train – just to sit on a closet that saves her pulling the chain . . . I've heard it all now!'

The two women ignored Jackson and continued to plan their visit.

By the time he returned from the fields, letters had been sent to both Sally and Lizzie informing them of the impending visit. Jackson knew that his cause was lost. He and Bill would just have to manage as best they could.

'Why couldn't you have waited until our Jane was at home?' he asked an excited and flustered Edith. 'Then we would have had somebody to make the meals and scald the milk tins . . . A chap has a job to manage every little thing on his own.'

His pleas fell on deaf ears.

'I can't remember you asking me if you could go to Penrith to buy a horse we didn't need, or to Cockermouth to shoot a few defenceless pheasants, leaving us to do all the milking on our own, Jackson. And, I'm not taking the pantry with me. There's plenty of cold meat and home-made cakes in the tins for you . . . What more do you want?'

'And the pub will still be there next week so you can complain to all your cronies,' laughed Esther as she packed her small suitcase.

The whole thing seemed like a conspiracy to Jackson. 'Since when have I eaten cold meat for a week? A chap keeps his family in luxury, only to see them flitting off for days on end, with no means of knowing whether he's alive or dead!'

* * *

The rocking, rumbling train slowly made its way south, stopping at every tiny station. Many platforms were so short that only part of the train settled over them. Should a passenger wish to get off but be 'marooned' beyond the platform, the train would obligingly edge forwards or backwards as required.

The West Cumbrian coastline is home to many hungry

flocks of gulls and oystercatchers, all flirting with the incoming waves, their prey first hidden, then momentarily revealed, enticing them to swoop down or dig and paddle in the soft sand. In places, the railway track runs so close to the edge of the cliff that the seats seem to sway into thin air. Only by pressing your face close to the window can you spot the reassuring fencing flicking by.

Sellafield with its pile chimneys – a new landmark for fishermen and land dwellers alike – soon came into view.

'Amazing,' said Edith. 'Who would have thought that such an important factory would ever be built in such a spot, so far from any town! But I suppose they know what they're doing.'

'I hope they do, Mam . . . But just look at the fells – the view is fantastic! I bet the workers have some smashing views from their windows.'

They were drawing into Seascale station.

'Look at that dining room,' gasped Esther. 'The Scafell Hotel always looks so inviting from the train. It's so close you almost feel you're intruding on someone's meal.'

'I prefer Ravenglass,' said Edith, as the train rattled across the viaduct towards the busy station.

'Yes, it makes me think of all the lovely trips we've had on the Ratty. I'm going into the corridor to see if I can catch a glimpse of it.'

Soon the train drew into Foxfield station where the two were to leave the coastal line and join the branch line to Coniston.

'I know Dad wanted us to go up Eskdale on the Ratty but riding in this train is something special,' said Esther, settling herself at the compartment window. 'It's so different from the coastal line . . . It's like journeying into an unknown land of mysterious hills and forests. There are so few villages and no signs of industry like on the line north to Carlisle. I'm always amazed at a station being named "Woodland" . . . and it's in a woodland!'

'That seems sensible to me.'

'I know, but it still sounds like a name taken from a fairytale.'

'It's starting to get dark,' said Edith. 'Sally said Jim's cousin Joe would meet us and walk up to the cottages with us . . . I said we could manage on our own but I'm sure he'll be waiting at the station. He wouldn't want us to find our way in the dark.'

At the end of the line, Coniston station had the air of a bustling metropolitan centre . . . the rush of steam hissed against the dome-shaped roof, announcing the train's arrival to the cluster of streets and houses at the foot of the hill.

Sure enough, it was quite dark now and the two women were relieved to see Joe waiting with his hurricane lamp.

* * *

Soon the trio had passed the Black Bull and were following a fairly broad path.

'We could have managed by ourselves, Joe. This path is clear enough for us to follow,' said Edith, feeling guilty about making Joe leave his comfortable cottage.

'It's no trouble, Edith,' he replied. 'The path is fine here where there is a good light, but further up you can easily miss your footing if you can't see clearly where you are going . . . Besides, I'm used to it. I could make the journey with my eyes shut. Many's the dark morning I've been so tired after a night out that I've made it to the quarry without remembering a step.'

Ten minutes later, Edith and Esther were very glad that Joe had insisted on accompanying them up the path.

As they gained height, the blackness wrapped itself round them, almost blotting out the light from the swaying lantern. Sky and moutain had merged, and the flickering light from the lamp revealed only a foot or so of the silvery, wavering path ahead.

The ledge on their right-hand side dropped down to the

tumbling waters of Church beck. During the friendly daylight its roaring descent was a source of delight and wonder, but in the blackness of night it was a menacing torrent threatening to draw the careless into its crashing depths.

Now I know what it must be like to be blind, thought Esther. Everything sounds louder than it should.

I shouldn't be frightened, thought Edith, as she concentrated on keeping up with Esther's hurrying heels. If she lost sight of them she would be left behind in the darkness. Joe was used to walking uphill at this pace – he didn't realise how hard it was for the two women to keep up with him.

'I'm looking forward to waking up tomorrow morning and seeing Coniston Old Man out of the window . . . Few people can have as good a view as Sally. Visitors come here from all over the world to enjoy the walks and views. It must be great to live in such a popular place,' said Esther bravely, eager to be sociable.

'It wasn't very popular with our Jim when he fell down the mountain and was lost in the snow, on his way back from Spying Cop Quarry,' said Joe amiably, without gasping for breath like Esther.

'He was missing for two days. They'd given him up for dead . . . but he was spotted, one foot sticking out of the snow. It was lucky anybody saw him. George Coward got an award for organising that rescue, and a lady called Marie Usher wrote a poem about it. Just imagine being buried all night up in these mountains!'

Edith shivered at the memory of the incident. Sally had thought she would never see Jim again. Only now, as they made their way up the inhospitable mountain track, did she realise how terrible it must have been for him.

'Yes,' continued Joe, as if he was chatting in his own front room, 'it's heavy, dangerous work. Walkers can choose when to go up the mountain but if you work here you have to go up, whether it's stormy or not . . . It had

snowed while we were in the quarry and we had no idea what depth it was when we set off for home.'

Joe opened a gate which barred their way and shone the light for them to pass through. Thankfully, it was only minutes before they reached the bridge over the racing beck.

'I think I can see a light in Sally's window,' cried Esther, relief flooding through her. 'And there she is, looking out for us!'

The welcome light streamed out of the open doorway.

'I'll set off back home now. You can see your way easily enough . . .'

As they turned to thank him, only the disappearing beam from his lamp betrayed Joe's progress back to the village.

*   *   *

'All the way to Coniston, just to use a lavatory that has no chain . . . You'd never believe anybody could be that daft.'

'I think you probably didn't hear what they said properly, Jackson,' laughed Mary Graham as she placed a portion of shepherd's pie on his waiting plate. 'It's a long time since Edith's visited her relatives in the Lakes . . . I wish I had a cousin I could visit in Coniston. I've heard it's a beautiful place. But it's a bit awkward to get to, what with changing trains and suchlike . . . It's easier to go to Keswick for a day.'

She turned to Tom. 'It's ages since we had a day in Keswick, Tom. Now that the weather's getting better, maybe we could have a trip out.' Mary sounded wistful.

'There you are, Tom. It just takes one of them to get a bit restless . . . and the whole district wants to be on the move!'

'Aye, and at ploughing time, Jackson. Wouldn't you think they'd decide to go round about January or February when little is going on?'

'Women seem to get these urges to wander about in the spring, Tom, just like them wintering Herdwicks who seem to smell the fresh grass miles away on their home fells.'

'It would take a pretty high dyke to keep a wandering wife at home, eh Jackson?' laughed Tom.

'Maybe good "grass" at home would make us settle a bit better!?' retorted Mary.

'There's not enough work to keep them busy at home these days . . . That's the reason,' asserted her husband.

'By God, Tom, you've hit it on the head. Our Esther said she fancied spending a few days without electricity, and sitting on a closet halfway up the fellside! You're right, we've spoilt them . . . Would you pass that bottle of sauce, Mary? It goes fine on this pie.'

'Aren't they going to spend a day or two in Ambleside as well, with your Lizzie?'

Jackson looked pained. 'Aye, there's no end to their gallivanting. And you might think that Ambleside is on the way home, but no . . . They've bought return tickets, so they'll have to come back the way they went!'

'Never mind, Jackson. It will have done them good,' observed Mary. 'Everybody needs a holiday from time to time.'

'I can't see why . . . It would be a bad day for the stock if Tom and me decided to catch a train and tour the countryside. Where would the money come from to pay for all their extravagances, eh Mary?'

Mary had already gone to the scullery to finish the washing up.

'It isn't as if she's visiting the most interesting of her relatives,' Jackson observed thoughtfully.

'Who should she visit?' asked his friend.

'A year or two ago, she decided to go and see her other cousins in Millom. A lot of her family live in Millom and Haverigg . . .' he explained.

179

'What was so much better about that visit then, Jackson?'

'They have more fun down there. One of Edith's cousins was telling her about the day they had to kill a bull.'

'Can I fill your mug, Jackson?' asked Mary, returning.

'Aye, thanks,' he said. 'Another piece of that apple cake wouldn't go amiss either, Mary.'

The plate was handed to him as he continued his tale. 'Apparently they were busy in the slaughterhouse and there was this bull to kill. So they tied it up by its ring and the butcher went to block it. (No humane killing in those days, as you know.) Well, the bloody thing decided to toss its head at the very last minute, and it was only half knocked out.'

'Poor thing . . .' gasped an astonished Mary.

'You like your meat don't you, Mary?' asked an impatient Jackson. 'Surely you don't expect the stock to commit suicide? Somebody's got to do the killing . . . If it was left to women, we'd all be a lot of sickly vegetarians.'

'Quite right,' agreed Tom. 'What happened to the bull then?'

'It panicked, tore itself free from its ring, which was left hanging on the wall, then it bolted out into the town.'

'How dangerous!'

'You bet it was, Mary. It raced from the slaughterhouse at the back of the Co-op, down Wellington Street, then saw that the Post Office door was open in Lapstone Road and in it dashed . . .'

'The folk inside must have got a shock.'

'According to our Edith's cousin, they were so surprised that nobody moved. They just watched as a ton of beef lumbered round behind the counter, then shot out of the shop and galloped on through the Market Square, over the railway bridge, up Horn Hill, to Haverigg, then waded out to sea. Now that's what I call a bit of real excitement!'

'Did they manage to catch it, Jackson?' asked Mary.

'Not bloody likely. It had too much sense to go back near

the slaughterhouse! It was washed up on the beach at Askham three days later . . . Now that's what I call an interesting holiday, Tom. The folk in Millom talk about that runaway bull to this day.'

Tom chuckled. 'I bet they didn't need to put salt on that beef!'

Mary looked disdainfully at the two men.

'How did they know it was the same beast, when it had been in the water for three days?' she asked. 'It could have been washed overboard from one of those Irish cattle boats.'

Jackson paused to consider the possibility . . . 'It had a Millom postmark on its back of course!' he smiled wickedly.

'The day I think anything like that is funny I'll know that something's wrong with me.'

'Oh, come on Mary. If you'd had to kill and butch as many animals as me, you'd be glad of a good laugh now and again . . . I could tell you a few more funny butching tales, believe me.'

'Well, don't bother.'

Jackson had a feeling it was time to make his way home.

*   *   *

The bus rocked and rattled along the twisting road. Esther was enjoying every minute of it. She glanced at the Skelwith Bridge Hotel, as they slowed down to allow some passengers to alight. Soon they were off, back to Coniston. It would be great to live in such a lovely area. Perhaps one day . . .

At last the bus drew to a halt in the centre of Coniston.

'We'd better hurry if we're to catch the train, Esther,' said her mother. 'I think I can hear it up in the station.'

To Esther, the mountains seemed to rise steeply from the edge of the village, then lean over, trying to shelter it from curious intruders.

181

Edith glanced at the Black Bull, and the path which had led them up to Sally's cottage . . . How she had enjoyed the few days with her family. Maybe she could visit them again next year.

At last they were seated in the train and they quickly left the Lakeland scenery behind.

Once they had boarded the north-bound train at Foxfield and begun their journey along the Irish Sea coast they felt they were truly on their way home.

'I wonder if your dad has managed to feed himself,' mused Edith aloud.

'Somehow I fancy he won't have starved, Mother.'

'Just so long as he hasn't gone begging food from any of the neighbours . . . That would put talk into their mouths!'

Esther laughed at her mother's worries. 'He would never need to beg from anybody . . . He has a way of appearing whenever there's a bit of spare food going! You mark my words, Mam, he won't be any thinner when we get home. In fact I shouldn't think he will have remembered which day we're coming back.'

* * *

Edith and Esther felt the warmth from the roaring fire as they entered the farm kitchen. Together with the two dogs, who were doing their best to wag their tails off, the blaze provided a fitting welcome for the two travellers.

'For a minute I thought it was a couple of intruders, the noise them two dogs made,' observed Jackson. 'They don't make such a fuss over folk they know . . .'

'We haven't been away that long,' laughed Edith. 'How have you managed without us?'

'I didn't remember exactly which day you said you were coming back . . . I've hardly missed you . . . and . . . Mary Graham makes a mighty fine shepherd's pie!'

'Well, I'd better get on with collecting the washing ready for tomorrow. There must be a good pile,' smiled Edith.

'I don't think there is any, Edith. I haven't changed my clothes. I've had a rest from all the fussing you do. I must say I've enjoyed this last week – a nice peaceful break.'

'There you are, Mother. I told you there was no need to worry . . . We can go off again next year!'

'Well,' said Jackson, reaching for his cap, 'seeing as everything is under control, I think I'll walk over to the pub and tell them that the travellers have landed back . . . I knew you would realise that there's no place like home, especially with all the modern luxuries we have here that haven't reached spots like Coniston yet!'

16

THE ROYAL VISIT

'Well, I thought she was beautiful,' Edith said, smiling at her sister across the tea table. 'I never thought the Queen would come to this part of the country.'

'If it wasn't for Calder Hall, she wouldn't have,' pronounced May. 'People like me who have lived in the south of the country are quite used to royalty of course . . .'

'Did she recognise you when she drove past?' asked Jackson wickedly.

'It was very good of her to come all this way.' Edith spoke quickly to forestall any unpleasant atmosphere that might result from Jackson's provocative comment.

Her sister continued as though Jackson had never spoken. 'In fact if I hadn't already decided to go shopping today I probably wouldn't have been on Main Street at all. Everybody up here makes such a fuss – it's easy to see that most people have little experience of town life, or any notion about high society . . . Could I have another cup of tea, Edith? I'm very peckish today, otherwise I would have waited until I reached home. You know . . .' Here she leaned towards her sister, her tone becoming confidential: '. . . the Queen drinks only China tea too. But it's rather hard to get it up here. I save mine just in case there is a shortage.'

Jackson looked up from his refuge behind the *Farmers' Weekly*. 'You just take a walk out here, May, when your pantry runs low. We're never short of tea or milk . . . There's nothing to beat a good half-pint mug of tea, especially if you've been spreading muck on stubble on a bitter, cold day.'

May quickly swapped her cup to her left hand, sipping

gingerly from the other rim as though wary of what might still be lurking on the surface.

Then, earrings glinting dangerously, she addressed Edith: 'As long as you're married to him, you'll never rise to anything better.' She wagged her finger towards Jackson who was studying the columns of his magazine, an innocent look just holding its own on his face. 'The minute you said he wore clogs, I knew you'd never have anything decent in the house.'

May finished the last few crumbs of her cake before continuing. 'Good tea *must* be sipped from a china cup. You can't do things by halves . . .' She nodded her head vigorously in Edith's direction to emphasise her point.

'Well now,' interrupted Jackson, 'your brother Alf is coming back from China or somewhere this week. Maybe he'll fetch us some china cups and China tea.'

'He's coming from Africa, not China.'

'It's all the same to me,' observed Jackson. 'I don't know the difference between them . . . All I know is that black folk live in Africa and yellow ones in China.'

May rattled her cup sharply into its saucer as her impatience threatened to spill over. 'The answer is gold! Gold!' Her voice rose defensively. 'Our family has worked in gold mining since the beginning of this century, Jackson Strong. My mother had a fleet of servants when she lived in Johannesburg. In those day it was only a small town, not the huge city it is today.'

'That's true, May. But your family were like a good many more . . . They went abroad to find work because there wasn't any here, and all they knew was mining, so they had little choice in the matter. To a hard-working miner there's no difference between coal, ore, gold or diamonds – they all kill.'

Edith's anxiety at the direction of the conversation prompted her to leave the table, hurry over to the dairy, and fetch a freshly baked apple cake.

'How about a piece of this apple cake, May? There's plenty of fresh cream to go with it.'

Her irate sister paused, the reply frozen on her lips. Her gaze rested on the proffered delicacy.

'That looks delicious, Edith.'

A brief, silent truce pervaded the tea table as cake and cream were served (generous portions had always been the hallmark of farming hospitality). And a further cup of tea lowered the tension to a level which Edith found acceptable. 'Yes,' continued May, as she settled herself in Jackson's armchair close to the fireplace, 'Alfred is bound to find a few changes when he gets home. He won't be used to manual work any more.'

'That's a pity,' remarked Jackson, trying to make himself comfortable in Edith's chair. 'I thought he'd be looking for work, so I was going to ask him if he'd concrete that second byre. The Milk Marketing Board like milk to come from concrete byres these days. They think our cobbled ones are dirty. (Not that that sort of thinking makes sense to me . . . After all, milk comes out of the cow straight into the milk tin. It doesn't have time to look around at the scenery.)'

'What daft things you say, Jackson,' snapped his sister-in-law. 'You can't really expect ordinary farmers to understand cleanliness and hygiene. Thank God we have a Milk Marketing Board to prevent us all from being poisoned in our own kitchens!'

'You didn't bother yourself about where that cream had been on its journey to your plate,' snapped Jackson.

'Everything in my kitchen is clean.' Edith's soothing voice was ignored by the two sparring partners.

'You're like a few more,' said Jackson. 'As long as you don't see the muck and the hard work, you'll eat anything . . . To hear you talk, anyone would think we'd swilled the byre floor down with the bloody stuff before we put it on your plate.'

Edith decided to divert the unfortunate course of this

discussion. 'Anyhow, it's been a very exciting week,' she began chirpily. 'Everybody has looked forward to the royal visit for such a long time, and they say it's to be shown on the television tonight. It would be nice to have a set . . .'

'I've lived through a good few reigns,' interrupted Jackson, not wishing to contemplate such an expensive outlay. 'You'll remember the old Queen's Golden Jubilee, May? There was such a lot of excitement throughout the country. I think we have a mug or something that was . . .'

'How old do you think I am, Jackson?' exploded May. 'Maybe *you* can remember things that happened before the turn of the century, but Edith and I certainly can't!

'We thought the old Queen would live for ever.' Jackson continued his reminiscences as though May hadn't contributed to the conversation. 'Folk couldn't remember a time when there was any other monarch. Tough old woman she must have been for those days, what with all them kids she had. Even my Uncle John worked his way through two wives before he had seven children!'

'How coarse you are at times Jackson . . . Royal ladies have servants to help them cope.'

'So long as they know when to stop helping . . .'

'The last few reigns have been very interesting,' interrupted a worried Edith. There was no knowing what offensive remark he might make just to upset May. 'We've been lucky to see so many coronations, we have a lovely display of mugs.'

She indicated the dresser as she spoke.

'Coronations are all well and fine,' said Jackson, ignoring his wife's comments, 'but the best thing that happened at the turn of the century was when Buffalo Bill visited Whitehaven . . . I was working up in Wasdale at the time. I walked all the way to Egremont one day, spent the night at home, then walked on to Whitehaven in the morning.'

'I've heard of that,' observed May, 'but it wasn't the sort

of thing that girls would go to watch. Rough lads, of course, enjoyed such wild entertainment.'

'Much too rough for the likes of you,' agreed Jackson sceptically. 'But it was a fine sight, watching the troupe arriving at Corkickle station. Then they galloped up the hill to Hensingham where the whole show was set up. There can't be anything on that new-fangled television to match that.'

'There's some good western films shown in Egremont picture house,' volunteered Edith who was a keen cinema-goer.

'Not a patch on the real thing, Edith. In the picture house all you can smell is the person sitting next to you. But we could smell the sweat and horse muck . . . And the tricks they could do on horseback were a sight to be seen. I shouldn't think there's ever been a show as good in Whitehaven. It's all rugby and pigeon racing these days.'

'Our Alfred has worked in Africa and America so I'm sure he's familiar with the native pastimes. Bill Cody is very famous in the States, or so I've heard.'

'Well, I suppose it'll come as a shock to him to see animals tied up in a byre, May . . . He will be used to either lassooing them to brand, or trapping them to send to zoos.'

'I'm sure our Alfred will be pleased to help you concrete the byre,' said Edith sweetly, afraid that her husband's sarcastic summary of their brother's activities would provoke a further outbreak of hostilities.

Jackson got to his feet and reached for his cap, as his smartly dressed sister-in-law opened her mouth to reply. 'Well, May,' he said, 'the Queen may come and the Queen may go, but it makes little difference to our lives.'

'That's an unpatriotic point of view, Jackson. The Queen sets a good example to all of us.'

Jackson smiled wickedly. 'I suppose we'll all start to drink China tea now eh? Somehow whatever goes into my half-pint mug tastes just as good after a dry day in the fields no matter what it is – tea or rain water. It's only upper-class folks who bother about different tastes. The rest of the world – that is the half that works for a living – just needs good wholesome food and a decent drink at the end of the day. The aristocracy have always been the same – they don't know what to think up next to pass the time away.'

Stick in hand, he made for the kitchen door.

'I think your Jackson's getting too old and set in his ways when he can't take an interest in a royal visit!' exclaimed May, carefully placing her fashionable hat on her permed hair, then bending forward to check her appearance in the small kitchen mirror.

'Take no notice of him, May,' replied her sister, reaching for the newspaper and holding up the front page which showed a large photograph of the Queen opening Calder Hall. 'Just before you came Jackson said, "We'll have to

189

keep this paper, Edith. It's not often we have royalty coming all this way to see us.'''

May looked puzzled. 'Why didn't you remind him of what he said earlier, Edith? He seems to say one thing one minute and another thing the next.'

'Well, May, you know as well as I do that men are difficult to understand at the best of times . . . Come on, I'll walk you as far as the bus stop.'

* * *

The same evening, as Jackson latched the chain on the yard gate, the sound of footsteps reached his ears.

'Hello, Tom, where are you off to?'

'I thought I'd spend an hour or so in the Grey Mare – I'm sick and tired of hearing about how lovely the Queen is, and how lucky we are that she found enough time to come all the way up here.'

'Then, it's what a lovely coat she wore, and how nice her shoes were . . .' agreed Jackson 'It was the same in our house. I was pleased to get out and milk the cows.'

'Why don't you come to the pub with me then?'

'Not tonight, Tom. I've a cow to calve so I'd better keep an eye on her.'

'By the way, I saw Edith's sister this afternoon, haring up the road towards the bus stop. She's a smart-looking woman, Jackson. Don't you think you picked the wrong sister?'

'Well now, Tom, it's a bit like choosing between a Clydesdale and one of them flashy Arab mares. One's dependable and biddable and the other's a bit too keen on head shaking and bridle rattling.'

'See you on Sunday night then,' said, Tom chuckling to himself. He wondered what Edith would have said if she'd heard her husband's summing up of the difference between her and her sister!

17

NEW JOBS FOR OLD

It was dark and very cold as Jackson hung his jacket on the peg behind the back door. Warmth and a good smell reached him from the farm kitchen.

'Supper ready?' he asked, settling into his favourite chair near the fire. 'That smells good, Mother. Since our Bill's started working at Sellafield, the milking is taking me much longer, so I'm certainly hungry . . . What have you made tonight?'

'You needn't feel hungry yet, Jackson. The supper won't be ready for another hour.'

'Another hour?' exclaimed the irate farmer. I've never had to wait for my supper before! What's made you so far behind with your work today? What do you think I spent all that money getting electricity put in for? I thought I was making life easier for you. But no, I've got to wait until you make up your mind to switch it on!'

'I'm waiting for Bill to come in from work, and then Esther, so we can all eat together. His train doesn't get in until half-past five, and he has to bike all the way home . . . Poor lad, he'll be cold and hungry, and ready for a nice rest and a good hot meal when he gets in . . . He left home at half-past six this morning.'

Jackson mimicked his wife's fussy tone. ' "Poor lad, he'll be cold and hungry, and ready for a nice rest . . ." And what about an old man like me being hungry, tired and ready for a rest?'

Edith ignored her husband.

'You don't work hard for somebody else. You can just rest while you wait, but poor Bill has to do what a boss wants him to do all day. He can't sit down and have a crack with anybody who happens to be passing by.'

'Work hard for somebody else?' echoed an astonished Jackson. 'What hard work? He goes out in the morning wearing a tie, a suit and a pair of shoes – not even clogs!'

He wagged his finger at his wife. 'Haven't you noticed that when he gets home his hands are cleaner than when he set off? You can't tell me that anyone who does a decent day's work can stay as clean as that.'

'You are silly, Jackson. Sellafield isn't a dirty factory in the same way as the pits and farms . . . No, this new sort of factory is clean. He tells me they have to change all their clothes and have a shower before they come home.'

'The only shower I ever had when I worked down the pits was what fell out of the sky as I walked home.'

'This dirt is a sort of dirt you can't see . . . Bill tells me they have to measure it on a special machine which tells them if they are clear of contamination or if they have to have another shower.'

'Sounds daft to me – I've never needed a machine to tell me I should wash.'

'Don't talk to me about it, Jackson,' Edith answered tartly. 'All I know is that he gets a decent wage and can afford to pay me money for his keep and . . .' Here she turned towards her husband and spoke very pointedly, 'that's more than he could ever do when he worked at home.'

She turned round to check the oven.

Jackson, however, was getting ever more indignant. 'I couldn't afford to give him a decent wage? Of course I couldn't. Taxpayers don't pay *me* good money to pay my workers – like they do at Sellafield. Oh no, I can't rival any firm that pays its workmen to wash off muck you can't even see. I work hard for my money – it's not just handed to me to throw away on anyone who chooses to turn up at the gate.'

'They don't just turn up at the gate. It took about six months before Bill was cleared by security. You must remember that nice man who came and asked such a lot of questions about the family?'

'I remember you saying something about it. It's lucky I wasn't in the house that day. Fancy coming to see if we're suitable!' Jackson poked the fire reflectively. 'It's a good thing the chap didn't ask *me* any questions . . .'

'I'm pleased about that too!' laughed Edith. 'As it is, he was accepted, just as Esther was . . . But if he had asked you any questions it might have been a different story.'

Jackson's face registered astonishment. 'What could *I* have said? A man like that has to be told the truth, Edith. If he'd asked me about my family, I would soon have told him that we have lived here for generations. The Strongs were probably living here before the Normans built Egremont Castle . . . Where did the Normans come from, Edith?'

'Normandy, I suppose.'

'What country is that in?'

'France.'

'You're right. I could have told him that the last lot we let in were the French in 1066 . . . but it won't happen again.'

'What on earth are you talking about, Jackson? You would have confused the poor man. At least I know not to take any notice of you. He would have been obliged to make a note of what you said.'

'Everything I've said would be important for a security man. Women don't understand international politics and security.'

'We don't? Well what has Egremont Castle got to do with all this security then?'

'Nationality,' explained Jackson patiently. 'You may have forgotten that we have just finished winning a world war. We, the English, won it . . . If this government has decided that this part of the country is the place to build a high-security atom factory, then I can well understand

them worrying if Germans, French – or any other foreigners – might try to get on the payroll. They are making sure
that we are all proper Englishmen. And . . .' He struck his
fist on the arm of his chair to emphasise his point, '. . . if
they came to check whether we are English – and
trustworthy – I could have told them that we have no
foreign blood in our veins . . .'

Edith continued to lay the table throughout her husband's monologue, knowing that eventually, lacking an
audience, the flow would run dry.

'Come to think of it, we kept the Scots out for long
enough, with their thin, scraggy cattle. I'm telling you
Edith . . .'

He struck his fist again on the corner of the table and the
cutlery sprang to attention. 'Adrian – that's the one – he
had the right idea . . . He built a wall to keep the Scots out.'

'You mean Hadrian.'

'Do I? A pity it was ever pulled down.'

'I'm glad that young man left before you came home.'

'Did he come from Sellafield?'

'No, from somewhere down south.'

'Down south? Down south?' Jackson's voice rose in
disbelief. 'A southerner! A foreigner! Coming here to see if
we're English?'

'Nobody doubts that we're English, but if a person wants
to work at Sellafield he should be of good character and
trustworthy . . .'

'Same thing,' retorted Jackson.

'The English can be thieves and criminals, just like any
other nationality,' replied his wife impatiently.

'Yes maybe, but no one asked if we were untrustworthy
when they sent out the call-up papers during the war.
Liars, thieves and downright lazy buggers were all wel-
comed into the fighting forces . . . They weren't so bloody
choosy then! Fancy having to fill in a government form to
decide whether we're fit to work in our own country. The
bloody Germans have more freedom than we have!'

'Just bend forward a bit,' Edith told him, 'and put a couple of lumps of coal on that fire before it dies . . .'

She glanced at the clock. 'Good heavens! He'll be here before long, I can't waste time listening to all this rubbish.'

* * *

'Well, how did it go today, Bill?'

'Fine, Mother. It's only training at the moment.'

'Your mother tells me they're teaching you how to wash off muck you can't see.'

'It's radioactive contamination, Dad. Not like ordinary muck – sort of x-rays that go right through you but you can't feel them.'

Edith looked alarmed. 'Oh dear! Are you sure it's safe?'

'So long as we do as we have been trained, it's OK. We wear factory clothes and have to spend ages changing and washing in the morning, at dinnertime and again after work.'

'It's a wonder you get any work done with all that changing. Of course you won't get paid for the time you spend in the changing rooms.'

'We do – it's all part of the job.'

'I wish there'd been easy work like that for me when I was your age, lad.'

'I reckon we're lucky, Dad . . . Somebody has to be lucky.'

Bill began to eat hungrily.

'My God!' exclaimed his father. 'You'd think you'd done a day's work, the way you're tucking into that dinner!'

Edith continued to serve the meal, exasperation written all over her face. 'There are many ways to work, Jackson. The country would be in a poor state indeed if there were only pitmen or farmers in it. Thinkers and organisers are just as important.'

Jackson nodded uncomprehendingly. 'That may be so, but I don't see why they should be paid more than the real workers in the country . . . We've always had to scratch a living as best we could.'

'Education is the answer, Jackson. A good scholar is the person of the future, you mark my words!'

Bill nodded. 'Mam's right. There's jobs galore at Sellafield for anyone with a bit of education, especially in the sciences . . . I wish I'd worked harder at school instead of wasting time with the lads.'

'It's no good thinking about that now, Bill,' said his mother. 'You were never as keen on schoolwork as the two girls. You can't make people into something they're not . . . I've learnt that from my efforts with your father!'

'I never thought you had anything to complain about as far as I was concerned,' retorted Jackson. 'Haven't I given you everything a wife could wish for?'

'Like what?'

'A fine farm, good stock, and I even had electricity put in – just for you.'

'You haven't benefited from the electricity?'

'No, not really. Milking by hand is a great way of checking on the condition of your cows. Nowadays farmers buy too many cows because they don't have the bother of milking them themselves . . .'

'What's wrong with buying a few more cows? I would have thought it was a good idea?' asked a surprised Bill.

'No, no, lad. The land can only stand so many cows grazing on it . . . Lazy farmers, who never like milking by hand, see an electric machine as a way of making more money the easy way . . . The land will be over-grazed, there won't be enough winter feeding and they'll soon have so many animals they won't even recognise their own stock . . . Factory farming I call it.'

'You have to have electricity nowadays, Dad. These new generating stations like Calder Hall will produce cheap electricity for everyone. You mark my words, this corner of the country will be a leader in the world of power.'

'Eh, lad. You talk like one of them chaps on the wireless

who say that coal is going out of fashion. Clean power for all of us . . .'

He turned to Edith. 'Isn't it marvellous, Mother? We've had a lifetime of bloody hard work. And if we'd only been born fifty years or so later, hard work would have been something that folk only read about in books.'

'I think you're both just talking about men's lives. I can't see that things will change much for women. Electricity doesn't do all the housework or shopping or manage the money . . . As usual, men will be the ones who benefit most from any new inventions.'

The door opened and Esther came into the kitchen, throwing her coat and bag over the nearest chair.

'Thank goodness you've got home before dark, Esther,' said her mother. 'Have you had a good day at work?'

'Have you ever heard such a daft question?' snorted her father. 'If our Bill goes to Sellafield to do damn all, then I'm sure Esther does a lot less . . . Them modern thinking chaps down there treat women as though they're something special.'

'And of course we aren't,' laughed Esther, sitting down at the table and attacking her supper.

'Your father has never thought so,' Edith remarked. 'We always came well behind a good working horse or a decent milking cow. Plenty of farmers have married a second or even a third time but thought twice about whether they could afford to tie up an additional cow in the byre!'

'Good money is hard come by, Edith. But there's always a queue of stong lasses on the lookout for a batchelor farmer or, better still, a widowed one.'

'I can't understand the logic of that, Dad. I'd want a husband who married me because he liked me or thought I was pretty.'

'I suppose that's what Sellafield does for local lasses now, eh Mother? They don't look at a chap to see if he can keep them. They know that a factory like that one can give any daft-looking lad a job for life! No lass, when your

mother looked for a husband she had to reckon up whether the chap could get a job that paid well enough to bring up a family.'

'Well I only just won through,' laughed Edith. 'There have been plenty of times when I've thought I'd drawn the short straw. And another thing, Jackson . . . I was as daft as any other lass. I married you because I thought you were the best-looking lad I'd seen. If I'd been bothered about how well you could support me then I'd have spent a bit more time looking around . . . 'She paused to reflect. 'In fact I don't think I'd have moved out of Whitehaven. There have always been good-looking, well-off chaps there. Maybe I should have spent a bit longer thinking about it!'

'Maybe you should have, Mother,' said Esther. 'But the young men working at Sellafield come from all over the country and most of them are both handsome and nice.'

'Don't you be taken in by any of them slick chaps from down south,' exclaimed a startled Jackson. 'They have smart ways of talking that can lead you astray ... A country lass like you has no idea what their homes are like. If they come up here to find a job it's probably because nobody'll give them one at home. You just be careful, my lass. You can't judge a parcel by its packaging.'

'Leave her alone, Jackson. She's a better judge of what somebody's like than you are. Girls are able to look after themselves these days.'

'Don't you believe it, Edith. Lasses were always a bit daft, and I reckon they'll always be swayed by the useless charmers of this world.'

'She can't go far wrong in the department she's working in,' volunteered Bill. 'They're all well-educated men there.'

'That's good to hear,' said Edith approvingly.

'In that case,' snarled a suspicious Jackson. 'a father like me will only be a handicap for an intelligent modern daughter like her.'

Esther glanced at her father and smiled mischievously. 'Don't worry, Dad. If I fancy any young chap I'll bring him home for your approval ... And if you don't like him I'll have to rethink, so don't start bothering yourself about the possibility of having "foreign" grandchildren just yet!'

'There you are Jackson,' soothed Edith. 'This new factory with its new way of living may well bring "foreigners" into the district ... But judging from some of the cantankerous local blood, it's bound to be a good thing ... You've often said yourself that a bit of foreign blood improves the stock!'

Both children laughed at the way their mother had turned their father's usual line of argument back on him.

Jackson looked hard in his wife's direction before he spoke. 'There's foreign, Mother, and *foreign*. Whitehaven is as foreign as is safe and decent. Any further afield and the mix is downright dangerous.'

Having made this declaration, Jackson got to his feet and reached for his cap and stick.

'Are you going to check the stock, Dad, before bedtime?' asked Esther, seeing her father move towards the door.

'No, lass, I'm off to the Grey Mare to have a good crack about old times before this foreign invasion from Sellafield turns our local pub into some sort of transport café!'

The family laughed as they heard the old man muttering to himself as he crossed the yard. Meanwhile Flash was racing ahead to reach the pub long before her master.